1968 107

keys
in our
hands

keys
in our
hands

Helen Kingsbury Wallace

THE JUDSON PRESS, VALLEY FORGE

". . . to every man his chance — to every man, regardless of his birth, his shining, golden opportunity — to every man the right to live, to work, to be himself, and to become whatever thing his manhood and his vision can combine to make him — this, seeker, is the promise of America."

(Thomas Wolfe in *You Can't Go Home Again*)

foreword

BEHIND ALL OF THE SOCIAL and economic conflicts of the civil rights struggle are dedicated, responsible, and concerned men and women of both races engaged in a quiet war against poverty and ignorance. Such a person is Miss Helen Kingsbury Wallace.

Keys in Our Hands by Miss Wallace vividly expresses her poignant feeling for the problems as she attempts to search our souls for understanding answers.

Keys in Our Hands has captured the pulse, emotion, and human interest of the plight of the minority group. *Keys in Our Hands* will perhaps introduce us to the questions and help find the solutions which will unlock the doors of truth and restore our faith in God.

LEON H. SULLIVAN

contents

preface

FAR FROM ASSUMING the position of an authority on problems of the underprivileged, I am satisfied to regard myself
as a mere observer of current events. In this book I am
trying to point out some of the projects that seem to me
to hold great promise for the future. These are simply
presented with the purpose of acquainting the average
man or woman with some current hopeful trends. If the
reader's point of view is broadened and his sympathies enlisted, the writer is content.

Most of the examples used are drawn from the city of
Philadelphia, where the author lives, where the Reverend
Dr. Leon H. Sullivan (some of whose many activities are
described) lives and works. But all of the projects men-

tioned are nationwide, rather than local, and are being tried in many cities across the land. This book is dedicated, with respect and admiration, to the Reverend Dr. Leon H. Sullivan.

Helen Kingsbury Wallace

Philadelphia, Pa.

the image
is a key

"HOLD UP YOUR HEADS; walk straight; be Somebody!" The speaker was a tall, dynamic Negro leader, the Reverend Dr. Leon H. Sullivan. He was addressing a convocation that had been organized to open in Germantown (a part of Philadelphia) a branch of the Opportunities Industrialization Center, familiarly known as OIC. Dr. Sullivan, pastor of Zion Baptist Church in Philadelphia, and founder and chairman of the board of OIC, was publicly expressing his deep conviction that the Negro's image of himself must undergo a change.

The often-used symbol of OIC is a key. Dr. Sullivan believes that one of the keys to doors now closed to Negroes is the Negro's *attitude*. He calls it a skeleton key because it unlocks so many doors. He believes that, as a first step, the Negro's attitude toward *himself* must change. He must create a new image of himself. He must gain self-confidence. One reason why the Negro lacks self-confidence is that he can see no future other than in servile jobs. He is unable to conceive of himself as participating in the main stream of life. He must be helped to believe in himself in order to achieve a career. He must learn independence, stand on his own two feet, and develop a new direction.

It is not difficult to understand why many Negroes lack self-confidence, causing some to be passive and retiring, and others to be belligerent and aggressive. Their background comprises years of actual slavery, years of oppression, and the denial of many basic rights. It is they who have done the world's hard, heavy labor, the unlovely tasks, the work that white men would not do. They have been treated as menials, herded in black ghettos, denied employment, and denied the right to vote. They have been given little opportunity for education, and what they received was often of inferior quality. Is it any wonder that they find it difficult to assume self-confidence and assurance, and to move freely in society as equals of white men? They must be granted the basic human rights: a job, education, housing, and the vote; such will give them the feeling of security. Only then can they take their rightful place in society. Only then can the Negro hold up his head, stand tall, and be Somebody.

Not only is the Negro's self-image a key to achieving a better relationship between the races. He must also change his image of the white man, and the white man must change his image of the Negro. Many whites are accustomed to thinking of Negroes in stereotypes: They like watermelon, let their property run down, and steal. These tendencies characterize some Negroes, but by no means all. Furthermore, they are true of some whites also. On the other hand, many white people do not realize that Negroes have just as stereotyped an image of them. Many Negroes believe that all whites hate Negroes, are exploiters, hypocrites, immoral, racists, and segregationists. These charges are true of some whites, but not of all. Each group must consciously change its image of the other before improvement in relations can take place.

In the Negro's image of the white man is a prominent dollar sign. Compelled to pay top prices for goods and services, the Negro might just as well be subjected to a color tax. Whites own the grocery and liquor stores in the Negro ghetto. Whites also operate the numbers racket and houses of ill repute. Exorbitant rentals for slum housing are charged by whites to Negroes. Absentee landlords make as much as 100% profit on poorly heated tenements and antiquated buildings, rat and roach infested. In these areas crime and juvenile delinquency flourish. The Negro feels that the white man keeps aloof, separated by zoning ordinances, little moved by the Negro's plight. He is content to be served by Negroes and willing that they should give their lives in the armed forces, but he wants no further contact with them.

The Negro notes that on election day the white candidate comes into the Negro community, backslapping, handshaking, perhaps dispensing beer, wine, and whiskey. On the following day all this cordiality recedes and is evident no more until the next election.

Mistrust, fear, and even hatred of whites dominate many Negro communities. The white image is associated with shooting, bombing, lynching, and raping. Negroes sometimes experience police brutality. Occasionally, because of beatings, they are forced to admit to crimes they never committed. Sometimes their trials in a so-called "court of justice" are pure mockery. In certain areas in the nation, the verdict of a case involving a Negro may be predicted in advance. In some Southern states the Negro rarely gets a fair trial and a just verdict. Roy Wilkins, executive director of the National Association for the Advancement of Colored People, states that in some Southern states no white person has ever been convicted of murdering a Negro. He adds that in the history of one Southern state, only Negroes have been executed for rape, though white men have committed the same crime.

But it is not only in the South that the Negro gets a bad deal. In the North, too, he is often discriminated against in regard to his basic rights: jobs, education, housing, and voting privileges. All of these facts are reflected in the Negro's image of the white man. The bitter hatred expressed in both North and South, symbolized by fatal shootings, beatings, bombed homes, burned churches, broken windows, the throwing of eggs and tomatoes, and the resurgence of the Ku Klux Klan can only sear an image of a white killer upon the Negro mind. This stereotype makes him suspicious of every white man who tries to help him.

Similarly, frequent robberies, rapes, and riots on the part of Negroes distort their image in the minds of whites. Mutual distrust stands as an obstacle to the establishment of a fine relationship. Both groups must come to realize that the unlovely images which both hold of each other spring from minority action and by no means represent all Negroes or all whites. Persons of each race must come to understand that a key in their hands is a *changed attitude*.

A very obvious need for a change of attitude is between

Northerners and Southerners. Present attitudes express themselves in prejudice and violence. Erskine Caldwell, in an illuminating article, "The Deep South's Other Venerable Tradition," in the *New York Times Magazine* of Sunday, July 11, 1965, describes Southern action based on hatred and expressing itself in violence:

> In an environment that for many generations has encouraged and condoned physical domination of Negroes, it was inevitable that the time would come when the attempt would be made to impose economic and political domination upon them lawfully or, if expedient, unlawfully.
>
> When lawful means failed, these white adults, gravitating into groups, did not hesitate to resort to unlawful means to try to prevent Negroes from seeking and acquiring their democratic rights. This is when violence erupts and where the use of guns, dynamite and flaming gasoline begins.[1]

And, it may be added, where retaliation begins as Negroes employ the same methods.

One of the saddest aspects of this hatred in the South is its inculcation by adults in their children, who are born totally without prejudice. Thus it is passed on from generation to generation. Few who saw them can forget the photographs of screaming mothers, their faces distorted by hate, urging their children to demonstrate against the Negro children entering an integrated school in the South.

Recently, a thoughtful Negro young woman, speaking of the Southern violence, said wholly without rancor or resentment, "It's the way they've been taught." Christian people in the North must try to match her understanding and forgiving spirit. And Northerners must remind themselves that hatred and violence characterize only a minority of Southerners.

In his article quoted above, Mr. Caldwell fully recognizes that not all Southerners are characterized by hatred.

[1] © 1965 by The New York Times Co. Reprinted by permission.

He says:

> A college-educated, younger-generation Southerner of Anglo-Saxon descent, mindful of the large accumulation of explicit pictures and records of the Deep South in the "Racial Sixties," is one of many who deplore and condemn the actions of those white Southerners who incite hatred and condone violence which in many instances lead to murder.
>
> This is the Southerner who is convinced that education and resulting enlightenment will eventually eliminate hate and prejudice, but he knows the process will take time for accomplishment.[2]

It must be borne in mind that the states most characterized by prejudice and hatred have been poor, rural states with a large number of uneducated persons of both races living in them. It is to be hoped that as the standards of education rise in these states, prejudice will decrease. Certainly many of the Southern states, while not sympathetic with the civil rights movement, have acted to enforce the law since the edict of the Supreme Court. It is equally certain that many Southerners deplore the violence that has taken place and believe that those guilty of it should be brought to trial.

Southerners are quite right in feeling that there are plenty of racial problems in the North, and one can understand the feeling of some of them that Northerners are blind "do-gooders" who ignore problems in their own backyards while they march in Southern protest movements. Some Southerners feel that reporters in the North are biased against the South, and that they give a slant to their news stories. Undoubtedly among many Northerners there is a tendency to create an image of Southerners as inspired by the violent minority rather than by the more open-minded majority. Certainly the North with its closed housing practices, its segregated schools, and its various

[2] Ibid.

instances of hateful treatment of Negroes, cannot afford to be too critical.

It is obvious that images on both sides need to be changed. More trust and mutual respect are needed.

Even the image of the Christian church needs to be altered. Fortunately the unchristian acts of many white churches in closing their doors to Negro worshipers are not typical of all white churches. But the Negro image of the white church is not flattering. In the eyes of many, efforts on the part of white Christians to fraternize are restricted to a condescending gesture on Brotherhood Sunday.

At the dedication of the Bright Hope Baptist Church in Philadelphia on May 2, 1965, Dr. Martin Luther King criticized the churches — including Negro churches — for failing to provide leadership in such social causes as civil rights. He said that the church is the "most segregated institution in America," and that eleven o'clock on Sunday morning is "the most segregated hour in America." He added that too many ministers "hide behind their stained-glass windows," and said that some churches are "the tail-lights instead of the headlights" in the effort for social improvement. "We suffer in this country," he said, "not only from the violence of the bad people, but from the silence and indifference of the good people."

"But," he said further, "there are signs that the churches are waking up." He then spoke of the large number of priests, nuns, and ministers who marched with the Negroes from Selma to Montgomery, Alabama.

To participate effectively in any kind of help, the white minister — indeed, the white layman — who espouses the Negro cause needs a knowledge of the suffering of the Negro community and a deep caring for Negroes. The white Christian must reveal to the Negro an image and a reality of love, concern, and helpfulness. Cooperation must replace paternalism in the white man, who must drop his sense of superiority, and arrogance. He must really acquire a feeling of equality — equality of birth, if not of achievement.

Some practical suggestions were advanced by Rev. Elder B. Hicks in the June, 1965, issue of *Crusader*. Dr. Hicks wrote that the churches can do much to change their image in Negro communities "by interracial home visits, pastoral exchange, inclusive church workshops, sharing in educational center teaching responsibilities, after-school tutoring to prevent dropouts, convention and associational visitation, youth exchange programs, inclusive vacation church schools, work for the implementation of the Civil Rights program which in itself involves education, housing, public accommodations, equal job opportunities, voting rights and the privilege of holding public office." Here are enough concrete suggestions for the churches, if they would take them seriously, to keep them busy for years to come!

Only by taking a position of leadership can the Christian church retain the respect of people. As Dr. King said, "Leadership must take the place of pious irrelevancy in the church; the church has too often been an echo rather than a voice."

Only when white people come to regard Negroes as men and women, human beings like themselves, having the same problems, the same aspirations and longings, the same faith and hope, entitled to the same rights, can a proper relationship exist between them. It is not enough to be "good to them." Negroes are not animals to be kindly treated; they are human beings to be approached on an equal footing. That many of them are not equals at present is because of their inferior background and opportunity. It is for the white man to provide opportunities that will produce equals. Already many Negroes — teachers, doctors, lawyers, and scientists — are on a professional level with their white colleagues. Illustrious names like those of Ralph Bunche, Marian Anderson, and Ira Reid, who have reached the tops of their professions, illustrate the inherent capabilities of the Negro.

As an illustration of what faith on the part of a Christian can achieve in changed attitudes, the following story of an effort made by the wife of Rev. Emmer Henri Booker when her husband was pastor of Jones Tabernacle (an African Methodist Episcopal church in the heart of the Negro community in Philadelphia) is offered. Mrs. Booker invited a group of teen-agers from street corners in the area into her home for a turkey dinner. The guests gave no indication of their familiarity with jails, truant officers, and knives. They were polite and respectful; their behavior was all that could be asked of guests.

Mrs. Booker explained to them why they had been invited.

"We're interested in you," she said. "Everything is open to you today — don't let it slide by. . . . You can become doctors, lawyers, ministers, fathers, all influencing other people. . . . Whatever you think is what you are. . . ."

"Man," said a 15-year-old to Dr. Booker, "this makes me feel like going straight."

a job
is a key

A STUDENT IN THE Opportunities Industrialization Center walked forty blocks and back every day to attend classes because he had no carfare. Some of the students cannot afford lunch, but they continue to attend the Center because they see in its program a solution for their problems.

Dr. Leon Sullivan is concerned with all the needs of underprivileged people. In the field of employment he has made a tremendous contribution by founding the Opportunities Industrialization Center, popularly known as OIC, in North Philadelphia, with branches in West Philadelphia, South Philadelphia, and Germantown, as well as a branch for Puerto Rican students. The purpose of these centers is to help students to *help themselves*. OIC leaflets

23

use the symbol of the key. Over it are the words "We help ourselves." OIC offers the uneducated and the unemployed the chance to learn needed skills, so that they may be qualified to apply for jobs, and so that they can hold the jobs after they get them.

Over 7,000 persons applied when OIC announced that it was accepting applications for training in skilled technical and service areas. At that time, the Center's capacity was about 300. Even with short-term programs, it could not meet the demand. Many institutions would have been pleased with such an opportunity to be selective. But the administration of OIC recognized and responded to the frustration that would be felt by thousands unable to get in. So they set up a Feeder Program in a former synagogue at Broad and Diamond Streets in North Philadelphia.

The people with whom they had to deal did not seem to be very promising. Many of the applicants were recent migrants from the South or from other rural areas. They had a low level of academic achievement and came from families that attached little value to education. During their all-important early years, few had been motivated toward learning. Many were victims of poverty and deprivation. North Philadelphia, where most of them lived, is characterized by high incidences of crime, school dropouts, slum housing, unemployment, juvenile delinquency, and illegitimacy. Aspirations were low, and so were the people's expectations of fulfillment.

OIC has brought a fresh approach to people on these low levels of achievement and hope. They know that low scores on tests will not cause them to be dropped. They know that their race or religion will not be held against them. They trust OIC's leadership. They are drawn to OIC because they believe in its concern and help. They know, too, that neither a lack of natural ability nor an inability to pay will be a barrier to enrollment.

Soon after OIC was founded, Dr. Sullivan said to a group of over 1,000 ill-educated, unemployed Negroes: "There are those in our community who believe that there's a segment of the population that isn't concerned with helping itself. We're going to prove here that what those people believe is a lie! You are part of an historic demonstration, and upon your performance in these next weeks will depend the futures of 20 million persons in our urban areas who have been brainwashed into thinking that they have inferior skills, inferior potential. . . ."

To meet the needs of these people, the Feeder Program of OIC was set up under a grant of $330,000 from the Office of Manpower of the U.S. Department of Labor. It feeds OIC, hence its name. Thousands who lack the necessary qualifications for immediate entry into OIC, or who are barred by lack of room at the Center, are prepared by the Feeder program for later entrance. Thus, valuable time is not lost and prospective OIC students are kept occupied until they are able to enter. The Feeder Program is a recruitment and prevocational program in basic instruction. It is designed to motivate, to stimulate, and to provide professional help in remedial education through guidance and counseling.

A staff director tells how the Feeder Program began: "It was soon apparent that among those students who were accepted into the [OIC] training courses there were serious deficiencies in the basic skills, i.e., reading, computational, and other communication skills. In other words, if these students could be exposed to a prevocational readiness program where screening, remedial education, and counseling could be done, their progress in the technical training would be greatly enhanced. It was also soon evident that many were ready to give up too soon. Some program was needed where the applicant's commitment to retraining could be made firm. The trainee needed to realize that learning usually comes as a result of a long, hard process, especially for an adult with poor educational foundations, attitudes, and motivations."

The administrator also spoke of the self-image: "The applicants must learn to hold their heads high, dress neatly, write legibly, be on time. In short, they must establish attitudes [that key word again] which either they never had, or which have been smothered by poverty and unemployment."

These are students who cannot attend other institutions because of their inability to deal with technical material, because they cannot pay tuition, and, above all, because of their lack of self-confidence. Some of them cannot even read. All of the teachers seek to search out the needs and weaknesses in their students and meet them with intensive training. Whether the student is deficient in spelling, arithmetic, manners, or grooming, he is helped to become more proficient and acceptable.

Classes meet for three hours a day, five days a week, for a twelve-weeks course. Three shifts attend each day: one from nine to twelve, another from one to four, and a third from seven to ten in the evening.

Many enrollees have been unemployed for so long that they lack courage to apply for training elsewhere. They come to OIC because they know that they will be welcomed, whatever their deficiencies. As one of the instructors in the Feeder Program put it: "Our purpose here is to help instill pride in these people, pride in their heritage. We want to develop attitudes toward themselves and toward whites that will enable them to improve themselves, get jobs, and perform well."

Some of the subjects offered by the Feeder Program are: Minority History, Job Finding, Grooming and Hygiene, Civil Service Opportunities, Effective Communication, Practical Mathematics, Reading, and Consumer Education. The course on Civil Service is among the most popular. Representatives of the Post Office, Internal Revenue Service, and other Federal agencies come to the Feeder Program to describe the opportunities for governmental service and help to prepare students for Civil Service examinations.

When students complete the twelve weeks, they are ready to go into intensive training classes at OIC or into other training opportunities. Some go into "on-the-job" training situations. Some move directly into full-time jobs from the Feeder Program. Many jobs are provided through the Manpower Automation and Training program.

Hundreds of job opportunities await Negroes who have the skills to fill them. Many new jobs are open to men and women, regardless of color. Doors formerly closed are now open. New kinds of jobs have been created by automation. Unskilled jobs disappear, but at the same time other jobs open up for workers who have special skills. More emphasis must be put upon preparation and training.

One-third of those enrolled in the Feeder Program of OIC are on public assistance. What draws them to this program? Probably this may be explained by the direct relationship between training and employment. Hundreds of persons formerly unemployable are now gainfully employed as a result of their studies. Then, too, there is the powerful personality of Dr. Sullivan. His sincerity and dedication attract a large following. He is not on the payroll of OIC. He regards his work there as merely an extension of his ministry at Zion Baptist Church.

The Feeder Program has 450 registered volunteers who serve as teachers, counselors, clerk-typists, and consultants. Among them are white students from Temple University.

A six-alarm blaze on July 17, 1965 destroyed the building where the Feeder Program was housed. All of the school's records went up in smoke, along with $20,000 worth of supplies and equipment. On that day, Dr. Sullivan said sadly, "This is a catastrophe for thousands of people who have pinned their hopes on this program. But this won't beat us. We will come back." And come back they did! With the approval of Governor Scranton of Pennsylvania, a large National Guard armory near the burned-out building was offered as a temporary home for the school. The fire occurred on Saturday evening. On the following Monday morning classes reconvened in the armory. Administrators began the colossal task of reregistering 5,500 previous, present, and future students.

Later, classes were temporarily transferred to rooms in Temple University. Now Feeder Program classrooms are in the building at 1225 North Broad Street which houses the OIC executive offices. Despite all of the frustration and difficulties, the Feeder Program has gone steadily on with no loss of students.

The Opportunities Industrialization Center itself grew out of a city-wide attempt under the dynamic leadership of Dr. Sullivan to reduce crime and juvenile delinquency. Some of the causes were found to be:

1. The breakup of the institution of the family, with many mothers heading families which are devoid of a strong father image.

2. The high, and still increasing, rate of school dropouts, throwing many more people into an already glutted labor market.

3. Inactivity among youngsters unable to find jobs or outlets to occupy their leisure time.

The first attempt to meet this problem seriously was the North Philadelphia Youth Community and Employment Services. An anonymous contribution of $36,600 was made to the project. It was housed in Zion Baptist Church, of which Dr. Sullivan is pastor, and had as its director the able Rev. Thomas J. Ritter, who later became administrator of OIC, and who is regarded by Dr. Sullivan as his strong right arm.

In spite of great efforts with this earlier program, disappointments developed. It was discovered that its 6,000 applicants faced closed doors when they sought employment. This was partially because of race prejudice, but also because the applicants lacked the skills and training to meet the requirements of industry.

A group of aroused Negro ministers — 400 of them — led a campaign to break down discriminatory practices by exhorting their congregations not to buy from companies where they were not permitted to work. Repeated victories brought a new respect for Negro leadership. Barriers against Negroes began to melt away. But then another obstacle became apparent. Unfortunately, when jobs in many classifications were opened to Negroes, too often men and women with the skills sought could not be found. Thus the need became evident for what was later to become the Opportunities Industrialization Center.

In the fall of 1962, serious talk of such a training program began. Early in the preceding July, a call had been issued for craftsmen and technicians who were familiar with the requirements of industry to meet at Zion Baptist Church. Over 100 persons, trained and employed in technical fields, assembled. Before the summer was over, more than 300 persons, Negro and white, had enlisted as volunteers to assist in the new program.

Next, industry's involvement was sought. Conferences with industrial leaders were held, the proposed program was described, and assistance was requested. Industry's response was immediate and favorable. Equipment was donated and ideas contributed.

Steps were then taken to establish a nonprofit corporation, the Opportunities Industrialization Center. An abandoned police station in the heart of North Philadelphia, unused for four years, was secured from the City Council for the payment of $1.00 a year. The building was in a most disheartening condition. There were water and dampness, holes in the floors, electric wires hanging, plumbing out of order, and walls crumbling. Rehabilitation of the building and the inauguration of the program began with a gift of $50,000 from an anonymous donor. Several companies, unions, foundations, civic bodies, and church groups gave additional support. The largest gift, in the amount of $200,000, came from an agency of the Ford Foundation: the Philadelphia Council for Community Advancement. The Ford Foundation has continued its generous giving of money, encouragement, and advice to the project.

OIC was dedicated on January 26, 1964. During May, 1964, a thousand volunteer "Opportunities Workers" conducted a Community Fund Drive and raised $102,000. A number of corporations, including Philco, General Electric, Budd Company, Sharpless Corporation, and Jerrold Electronics, donated over two hundred thousand dollars' worth of equipment. The basic philosophy underlying OIC is that of a program "predicated on the belief that the ultimate salvation of depressed communities depends upon the organized, creative, and purposeful efforts of the people within the communities themselves, lifting themselves and helping themselves, with the assistance of government, industry and philanthropy." OIC is "an attempt to prove that it is possible to take the raw materials of humanity, both colored and white, off the street corners" and enable them to become "productive citizens and skilled workmen."

The North Philadelphia Branch of OIC offers training in restaurant practices, commercial cooking, chemistry laboratory techniques, sheet metal work, teletype, power sewing, machine tool operation, and electronic assembly.

The Germantown Branch offers courses in laundry and dry cleaning, power sewing, plumbing, refrigeration, air conditioning and heating, brick masonry, the work of the clerk-typist, and electricity.

The West Philadelphia Branch teaches merchandising-marketing, small business management, real estate sales, IBM key punch operation, the work of the electronics technician, computer technology, secretarial science, and office machine operation.

Another branch in South Philadelphia provides instruction in printing (cold composition), commercial art, the work of the clerk-typist, restaurant practices, commercial cooking, office machine repair, and industrial machine maintenance. A branch has been opened in Norristown, Pa., and others will undoubtedly be opened where the need occurs.

Thus each young man or woman who comes to OIC is offered a wide choice of opportunities. Each enrollee is required to take basic courses in the communication skills of arithmetic, reading, and the making of both written and oral reports. He can study consumer education, the civic understandings of politics, voting procedures, taxation, and the history of minority groups. There are frequent interviews.

The classes are "open to all persons, regardless of race, color, creed, and sex, for the purpose of motivating, developing, and utilizing the technical skills of people in the art of manufacturing and industrialization."

An effort is made to give each trainee a picture of what society expects of him and also what is expected of him in his chosen job. The effect of all this instruction upon his self-image is very good. He becomes involved in and committed to the philosophy and objectives of the program. OIC is concerned with the whole man — his head, his hands, his health, and his heart. This concern reaches into his home, enveloping his family and his contacts. OIC is committed not only to training the unemployed and the underemployed, but to building up the student's faith in himself and in others. Obstacles to the achievement of these goals seem almost insuperable. The trainee has to overcome poverty, poor housing, inadequate education, racial prejudice, and the lack of social acceptance. Nevertheless, the typical trainee *does* overcome.

The attempt to build up the student's self-image is helped by contacts made while he is taking the course. When visits to industrial plants are made, the trainee often meets other Negroes who, through hard work, have achieved success in the very field in which he, himself, is interested. He thus gains confidence and the ambition to do the same with his life. The young trainee who has been a juvenile delinquent breaks with his gang. He ceases to be a delinquent. New ideas, a new way of life, and new training have wrought changes in him. The new attitudes, the new image, and the new job are keys to a better life.

At present the unemployment rate among Negroes is about double that of whites. Herbert Hill of the NAACP said recently as recorded in the *Christian Science Monitor:*

> "There have been symbolic breakthroughs for technical and professional Negroes. But this has had little meaning for the Negro blue collar worker, the Negro production worker."
>
> In fact, Mr. Hill said, the levels of unemployment and average difference in income between Negro and white workers is growing greater. . . .
>
> "The entire Negro community is on the edge of an economic crisis. Unemployment among Negroes is approaching the level of the Great Depression."

His solution:

> "There has to be a massive federally sponsored series of training programs for the millions of unemployed Negro workers—and white workers, too.
>
> "We also need some basic primary research in the requirements of the labor market in the future. . . ."[1]

OIC has made an exciting start toward solving the Negro's job problem. Here is a key that will unlock many doors. And what is being accomplished in Philadelphia can be reproduced in many cities throughout the country. Many cities have sent representatives to OIC to study its methods. Plans and programs for OIC are already under way in some of these cities.

---

[1] David R. Francis, "Negro Job Outlook," *The Christian Science Monitor,* April 1, 1965, © 1965 The Christian Science Publishing Society.

adult armchair education
is a key

A UNIQUE EXTENSION PROGRAM, related to OIC, has been devised by Dr. Sullivan. It is known as the Adult Armchair Education Program (AAE). The philosophy behind AAE is the same as that of its parent, OIC, namely, "We help ourselves." AAE is an opportunity for self-help which is carried directly to the people of Philadelphia, right into their homes. The dual purpose of AAE is basic adult education and community service. It has attracted considerable volunteer help.

In this plan a host opens his home to fifteen neighbors and friends for two hours a week over a period of ten weeks. An OIC staff teacher instructs them in basic subjects. As a result, many persons who have taken part in such groups seek vocational training at one of the OIC centers.

The atmosphere of AAE classes is informal and relaxed, because the meetings take place in homes conveniently located in the neighborhood where those attending live. The program reaches some who, for one reason or another, do not come to OIC. So OIC goes to them. And if an average of ten people meet in each of 150 homes, 1500 persons can be reached with the message of OIC.

The reasons why people are drawn to Adult Armchair Education are varied and numerous. Some wish to improve their computational and communication skills. (This is another way of saying that they want help with such essentials as arithmetic, spelling, grammar, and speech.) Some want to know more about minority history. Others want consumer knowledge — how to buy wisely. Some want help with voting or taxes. Some come merely from curiosity. Still others like to get together with friends and neighbors socially. In order that interest may be sustained, teachers emphasize that the program's real purposes are basic adult education and community service.

Seven fundamental goals are sought by AAE:

1. To develop a program of basic adult education presented in the informal atmosphere of the home.
2. To motivate unemployed and underemployed trainees in AAE to begin job training at OIC.
3. To assist trainees in finding jobs so as to relieve their immediate financial problems.
4. To provide counseling and referral services in the neighborhood.
5. To discover leadership potential in trainees and channel it into constructive outlets for the help of the community.

6. To provide an opportunity for participation in group discussions as a starting point for constructive group activities.

7. To maintain a flexible program which can respond to the expressed needs and desires of the individual trainees.

These goals are realized through AAE leaders who are prepared to teach communication skills, mathematics, consumer education, minority history, and community problems with possible solutions. These are the five major areas of education and discussion. The division of the available time is determined by the leader, and he must be flexible enough to satisfy the trainees' needs.

He must also create an atmosphere. He must achieve an informal, relaxed situation by being fully at ease himself, by injecting humor where it is appropriate, and by trying to bring out the ideas of each member of the group so that each one feels that he is a part of the procedure. He must help each trainee to express himself without embarrassment or self-consciousness. He must convey to each member of the group that his purpose is to help. He must ease any apprehension on the part of the trainees and help them to feel that they are learning together and are aiding one another to advance as far as possible. Improvement may not be miraculous, but if each trainee advances a little and has a revived appetite for improvement, much may be achieved. The goal is to inspire trainees to continue their self-help, by going on to attend OIC, by referral to community school programs, or by participation in spin-off activities. The last-mentioned are constructive activities of AAE classes. For example, an AAE class decided to take as its community project the obtaining of a school crossing guard for a dangerous corner. After they had made a contact with the proper authorities, an inspection was made. Then, in addition, a member of the AAE class passed the required test and became the new crossing guard. Another class has succeeded in getting abandoned cars removed from the neighborhood by sending a flood of letters and making many telephone calls.

Still another AAE class, attended by students who all live in the same apartment house, chose as their community problem the formation of a building management committee. Under the guidance of an able volunteer from the federal VISTA program, the group succeeded in correcting many abuses in the management of their building. They were pleased to see improvements brought about as a result of working together and helping themselves. Moreover, they were surprised to discover leadership qualities that they did not know existed in members of the group.

Spin-off classes have been organized to engage in specific areas of instruction, such as sewing, which are not a part of the usual AAE curriculum but are desired by a group of trainees.

Each teacher of an AAE class must present a clear picture of what OIC is, how it works, and what courses are available. He must encourage trainees who become interested in OIC to apply for enrollment. Applications of AAE trainees receive top priority.

The AAE teacher will come upon trainees who have pressing financial obligations which can be met only through jobs. The teacher will then give these trainees' names to an AAE supervisor. Similarly, other problems which are discovered are communicated to OIC's staff of counselors and social workers. Some trainees will exhibit talents and leadership potential which can be utilized for the good of the community. Potential leaders will be encouraged to attend conferences in certain homes devoted to teacher-training leadership, a part of the AAE program. They will be used in the AAE program and in the area of community development, according to their talents.

Sometimes persons who have been trained at OIC develop an interest in AAE and take an active part in it. The hostess of an AAE class is a former graduate of a power machine class at OIC. She successfully completed two hundred hours of training. She has received numerous offers of jobs and is presently working at her new trade. Once a week she opens her home to others, hoping to help someone else in some way.

A young man in an AAE leadership class, also an OIC graduate, plans to enter Wilberforce College in the fall. In the meantime, he is preparing to become a discussion leader in an AAE home, where he can help and encourage others.

AAE classes prove to be both successful and popular. Several groups, at the close of a ten-weeks session, asked if they might continue in a second session. One group was so interested in improving basic skills, so much impressed with the helpful attitude of their discussion leader, and so involved in the discussion of community problems that it maintained perfect attendance throughout the entire ten-weeks period. There seems little doubt that OIC has a good thing going in AAE.

the vote
is a key

On Sunday, March 7, 1965, about five hundred Negroes left Brown's Chapel in Selma, Alabama, planning to march fifty miles to Montgomery, the capital, to dramatize their complaints against the refusal to register Negroes as voters. Governor Wallace viewed the march as illegal and was determined to break it up. Under the direction of Sheriff James G. Clark, state troopers and deputy sheriffs of Dallas County halted the marchers as they crossed the bridge over the Alabama River in downtown Selma and commanded them to disband within two minutes. Instead of complying immediately, they paused to pray.

On order, fifty state troopers then advanced upon them. Sheriff Clark's deputized, mounted posse rode into their midst from behind them. Tear gas, whips, and clubs were used. The marchers retreated to Brown's Chapel and were sent to their homes by the sheriff and his deputies. Sheriff Clark wore a button on his lapel with the word "Never" on it. About fifteen of the marchers were hospitalized, and over thirty others received treatment for lesser injuries and the effect of tear gas.

On the following Thursday, March 11, the Rev. James J. Reeb of Boston died from multiple skull fractures received on Tuesday night when four white men attacked him and two other visiting clergymen who had come to support the marchers. Three of these alleged attackers were acquitted. The fourth was never indicted; he was only called as a witness against the other three.

President Lyndon B. Johnson, speaking to Congress on March 15, said: "At times history and fate meet at a single time in a single place to shape a turning point in man's unending search for freedom. So it was at Lexington and Concord. So it was a century ago at Appomattox. So it was last week in Selma, Alabama.

"There, long-suffering men and women peacefully protested the denial of their rights as Americans. Many were brutally assaulted. One good man — a man of God — was killed."

On March 11, Senator Hugh Scott of Pennsylvania, addressing the Senate, asked: "How can a nation hold its head high as freedom's leader among the peoples of Southeast Asia when it allows its citizens to be beaten, gassed, and flogged in its streets because they want to vote, and when a minister of the gospel is beaten almost to death?" (Senator Scott spoke before the death of the Rev. James J. Reeb was known.)

On March 21, Dr. Martin Luther King, Jr., Baptist minister and president of the Southern Christian Leadership Conference, led thousands of followers and sympathizers out of Selma on a five-day march to Montgomery. Many churchmen marched in response to Dr. King's call for help. Also in the line were students, motion picture stars, teen-agers, and field hands. Dr. Ralph Bunche, United Nations undersecretary for special political affairs, marched at Dr. King's side.

Security for the marchers was assured by three thousand troops, including 1,863 federalized Alabama National Guardsmen called to active duty, 509 Regular Army troops in the immediate area, five hundred troops at Montgomery, and a thousand standing by at Fort Benning, Ga. One hundred FBI agents and seventy-five United States marshals were there. Also on hand was a large force of State police. Brigadier General Henry V. Graham, of Alabama's 31st National Guard Division, was in overall command. A federal court order enjoined Governor Wallace and other state officials from interfering.

An issue far greater than the original one had been joined. Negroes of Selma had been denied their constitutional right to register and vote, but these injustices, grave and deplorable as they were, had now become symbolic of all the indignities inflicted upon Negroes wherever prejudices prevail.

Spurred by this demonstration and the awakening conscience of the American people, the Congress passed the federal Voting Rights Act, and it was signed into law by President Johnson on Friday, August 6, 1965. Literacy tests and similar voter qualification devices were automatically suspended in any state or county which used them on November 1, 1964, if less than fifty percent of the voting-age residents were registered on that date or voted in the Presidential election of 1964. Areas affected were Alabama, Alaska, Georgia, Louisiana, Mississippi, South Carolina, Virginia, an estimated thirty-four counties in North Carolina, and one county each in Arizona, Idaho, and Maine.

The Civil Service Commission appointed trained examiners to register voters in any county covered by the test suspension if the Attorney General received at least twenty valid complaints of voting discrimination, or if he decided it was necessary to enforce the Fifteenth Amendment.

The Attorney General was directed to file suits to challenge the constitutionality of poll taxes which were still required of voters in state and local elections in Alabama, Mississippi, Texas, and Virginia. The measure included a Congressional declaration that in some areas the right to vote was denied or abridged by requiring poll tax payments as a condition for voting. The federal Voting Rights Act took effect immediately. It applied to federal, state, and local elections, and also to elections for party offices.

Civil Rights leaders anticipated that there would be a great increase in the number of voters and thought that the Voting Rights Act would eliminate official discrimination in registration procedures. When the federal registrars opened their offices for business in Alabama, Mississippi, and Louisiana they met prompt and enthusiastic response. Thousands of Negroes came forward to register. One hundred thousand registered in five weeks. It was ample proof that there was a need for such action.

Notwithstanding the fact that thousands of Negroes were registered, two major hurdles remained: economic reprisals and violence. Dr. King believes that the economic threat is the greater problem. Although bombings, church burnings, and killings draw more attention, economic reprisals are more widespread. The rabid racists who deal in violence are comparatively few. But thousands of bankers, merchants, and other powerful figures who are segregationists deal in economic reprisals. Scores of Negroes are fired from their jobs by white employers. Or they discover that their credit is no longer good, or their insurance has been canceled. Hundreds of Negro sharecroppers who took part in registration drives have been evicted from farms. Dr. King has been considering pressing for a law to provide a federal subsidy for anyone who loses his job because of registration efforts.

President Johnson, in his message to a joint session of Congress on March 15, 1965, said: "Many of the issues of civil rights are complex and difficult. But about this there can be no argument. Every American citizen must have an equal right to vote. There is no reason which can excuse the denial of that right. There is no duty which weighs more heavily on us than the duty to ensure that right. Yet the harsh fact is that in many places in this country men and women are kept from voting because they are Negroes.

"Every device of which human ingenuity is capable has been used to deny this right. The Negro citizen may go to register only to be told that the day is wrong, the hour is late, or the official in charge is absent. If he persists, and manages to present himself to the registrar, he may be disqualified because he did not spell out his middle name or because he abbreviated a word on the application.

"If he manages to fill out an application, he is given a test. The registrar is the sole judge of whether he passes this test. He may be asked to recite the entire Constitution, or explain the most complex provisions of state law. Even a college degree cannot be used to prove that he can read or write.

"For the fact is that the only way to pass these barriers is to show a white skin."

It was just such injustices that the federal Voting Rights Act was intended to eliminate. In many cases, it has. It was not a figment of imagination that such an act was needed. It is now for courageous and enlightened Southern leaders to take a stand for the rights of American citizens to vote without being stopped because of racial discrimination. As this conviction and resultant action spreads, we shall hear of fewer bombings and church burnings, fewer murders by night riders, and fewer credit withdrawals and evictions.

As we have seen, the nonviolent demonstration is a key in the hand of the Negro. By using it he has dramatized his lack of the basic human right to vote. By using it he has gained registration rights for thousands. After he has secured the right to vote, the vote itself is a key in his hand, just as it is in the hand of the white man. But he needs encouragement to use it and guidance in how to use it effectively. He needs to be taught that it may be used to bring about the changes he wants and needs, such as better housing, schools, and health and welfare services.

The League of Women Voters Education Fund, established in 1957, "works to strengthen citizens' knowledge of the principles and techniques of representative government in the United States." It is financed through grants, gifts, and bequests from foundations, corporations, and individuals. The Fund has prepared a registration and voting manual entitled *Voting Is People Power,* for inner-city drives, available to people who want to use that power and help others to do so. The address of the Fund is:

1200 Seventeenth St., N. W.
Washington, D. C. 20036

The manual is comprehensive and easy to understand. It is based on several years of practical experience in reaching the citizens of the inner city in each of nine metropolitan areas in eight states. Under a grant from the Sears-Roebuck Foundation, the League of Women Voters Education Fund initiated projects to increase registration and voting by the "hard to reach" — especially Negroes, Puerto Ricans, and newcomers from Appalachia and other depressed areas.

The cities where the nine pilot projects were tried were Bridgeport, Conn.; Cincinnati, Ohio; Cleveland, Ohio; Indianapolis, Ind.; Milwaukee, Wis.; Detroit, Mich.; Long Beach, Calif.; New Orleans, La.; and Rochester, N. Y. Work was begun in Philadelphia, Pa., in 1965, and the League of Women Voters Education Fund has an office there at 1601 S. Broad St. Inner-city projects are also under way in Baltimore, Md.; Boston, Mass.; and Chester, Pa.

Registration and voting should be promoted on a *community* basis. In any given community, the political parties, labor unions, business organizations, civil rights groups, and other civic associations, the League of Women Voters, and the League of Women Voters Education Fund should all work together, all unite their efforts, to get out the vote. People have to be shown that their voices are silent if they do not vote — silent on pressing problems such as garbage collection, police brutality, rats, and discrimination. The vote has to be related to their needs.

Any person or group eager to share in this educational project can learn every step of organizational procedure by getting in touch with the League of Women Voters Education Fund and obtaining *Voting Is People Power*. Aristotle said: "If liberty and equality are chiefly to be found in democracy, they will be best attained when all persons alike share in the government to the utmost."

housing
is a key

As ONE RIDES OVER THE elevated tracks of the railroad leaving Grand Central Station in New York, he looks directly into Negro homes, and down into the teeming streets of Harlem. If he has any heart at all, he must be moved by what he sees: small children playing in the streets, adults sitting on the doorsteps or fire escapes and leaning from windows. There is not a tree or a grassy plot for them to enjoy. Harlem is a black ghetto to which many Negroes are committed for life. Apartments are filled to overflowing with human occupants — four or five, or even more, sleeping in one room. They are infested with rats and roaches. Toilets and washing facilities are extremely inadequate. What sort of life can a child have when he grows up in such surroundings? If one walks through North Central Philadelphia or Chicago's South Side, he sees the same conditions. The slums in the Northern cities are a national disgrace.

How may Negroes move out of these sections into decent communities elsewhere? They cannot move freely as long as white people strongly resist their entrance into such communities. Many people, both black and white, need to change their image of housing. Negroes are inclined to feel that they are safer in the Negro community. Many are too timid to seek housing in an all-white or even an integrated section. According to McKinley Farmer, housing representative for the Commission on Human Relations, Negroes have not done enough to open up the housing market. They often will not initiate entrance into new areas, he says, but rather will resign themselves to living in, or on the fringes of, racial ghettos. "Many Negroes are understandably fearful about trying to locate in a white neighborhood," he says, "even though that is where the majority of decent housing is to be found. They are reluctant to place their families in jeopardy. The stories they hear . . . and the treatment they receive from builders and real estate dealers encourage them to stick near the ghetto."

Whites, on the other hand, have fixed images of Negro neighbors. They believe Negroes let property run down and breed crime and juvenile delinquency. And, to be sure, there is some justification for these views.

But the image of a desirable potential neighbor is important for both whites and Negroes to achieve, and many whites and many Negroes answer this description. This is the key to decent housing, and decent housing is a key to the solution of many Negro problems.

It follows that each must then seek to live up to the image the other holds. Whites must lay aside their prejudice, their sense of superiority, and their preconceived ideas. Negroes must, through care for their property and neighborly attitudes, prove themselves desirable members of the community.

In his excellent documentary, "The Negro in Philadelphia," a supplement of the *Sunday Bulletin,* January 24, 1965, Joseph R. Daughen wrote: "The stoutest and stoniest wall that excludes the Negro is the one that surrounds the white man's neighborhoods, refusing entrance to him and his family." He added that in spite of legislation by the city council and the state and pressure brought to bear by the federal government's Housing and Home Finance Agency, new housing for the Negro is all but nonexistent. He said that even more restricted was the market for good older homes in established communities. "Except for a handful of deliberately integrated areas, the Negro seeking a home is forced to purchase where others of his race have already located," he said.

Some of the most flagrant illustrations of white resistance to Negro neighbors in Pennsylvania were instances in Levittown, Folcroft, and the Kensington area of Philadelphia. In 1957 the Negro family of William and Daisy Myers, who tried to move into Levittown, was greeted by stones. Later, some white neighbors repented of this occurrence, and the founders of the community issued the following statement: "We are ashamed of the terrible incidents that took place in our neighborhood during August and September. We feel that they have very seriously damaged the reputation of our community and of all Levittown."

On August 29, 1963, Horace and Sara Baker, Negroes,

tried to move into Delmar Village, an all-white section of Folcroft in Delaware County. Horace Baker was a laboratory technician; his wife, a nurse. When they arrived at their new home, more than 500 persons brandishing "Nigger, go home" signs and throwing rocks, tomatoes, and eggs, were there to meet them. Every window on the front of their house was broken. The rioting and maltreatment heaped on Baker and his family sent him to a sanitarium, split the neighborhood, and caused violent disputes between civic and religious leaders.

Early in October, 1966, whites threw bottles, rocks, eggs, and potatoes at the home of Mr. and Mrs. Leon Wright and their three children. Every window in the house was broken. The mob threw paint on some of the 400 policemen who were called out.

In the last few years a slight change in the attitudes of white people toward Negro neighbors was noted. George Gallup, director of the American Institute of Public Opinion at Princeton, New Jersey, said that in May, 1965, more white persons than two years before were willing to accept Negro neighbors. In a survey in May, 1963, 45% of whites across the nation said that they would move — or might move — if a colored family came to live next door. In May, 1965, the comparable figure was 35%. If Negroes in great numbers came to live in white neighborhoods, 69% of whites said in May, 1965, that they would move or might move. Two years before, 78% were in this category. In white opposition to Negro neighbors, this survey shows that the South leads, the Midwest and the Far West are about equal, and the least opposition is in the East.

Some responded to the question, "Suppose a Negro family moved next door to you. What would you do?" A machine operator in Tennessee replied, "I would just live here as usual. That's the trouble with whites — they panic too quick." A retired railroad worker in Pennsylvania said, "I would sell my home the next day." A California steelworker said, "It wouldn't bother me. If he can afford the same rent as me, he is entitled to live where he pleases." A Florida housewife replied, "If I couldn't live with it, I'd move out. Certainly it would depend a lot on the type of people. I wouldn't like it any better if poor white trash moved in. If they are clean and respectable, I don't feel I have a right to push them aside." "I wouldn't be too happy, but they might be better than what I have next door," said an Indiana wife of an automobile worker. An Oregon woman replied, "Wouldn't bother me a bit. If they could afford one of these houses, they must be pretty energetic."

Eighteen years after the Housing Act of 1949 set a national goal of decent housing and suitable living conditions for all Americans, over five million American families — one sixth of the urban population — are said to live in slums. Two undesirable results occur when the flow of Negroes away from slums is restricted. Neighborhoods where Negroes are permitted become overcrowded and form potentially dangerous sections. Then, because some localities are all white and others all colored, the city has *de facto* segregation in the schools.

North Philadelphia is home to more than a quarter million Negroes — almost half the Negroes in the whole city. In a survey of thousands of Negro residents in Philadelphia, the most pressing problem listed was housing. When a Negro tries to leave North Philadelphia, for example, by moving into a comfortable home in a white section, the owner or real estate agent puts incredible, often insuperable, objects in his path. Great persistence is required on the part of the Negro if his goal is to be achieved. Michelle Osborn, in the sixth of a series of articles on Negro problems for the Philadelphia *Evening Bulletin,* in the issue of January 9, 1967, quotes William Cameron of the Fair Housing Council of Delaware Valley as saying, "When a real estate guy tells you the key's been lost, or that nothing's available when he has listings, or that an apartment's been rented when it hasn't, or that the price quoted for a home advertised in the paper was a misprint and it's actually $6,000 higher, or the salesman hides in the closet of a house open for inspection — and these are all things that have actually happened — I call them acts of bad faith and dishonesty."

The Fair Housing Council has assisted some 400 Negro families to move into white neighborhoods over the last few years, but this is merely a drop in the bucket. To help meet the great demand for housing, Dr. Sullivan has organized the Community Investment Corporation. He began by organizing the members of his congregation in Zion Baptist Church into the Zion Nonprofit Corporation. This took place three years ago with what Dr. Sullivan calls his 10-36-50 program. He asked for 50 people who would agree to contribute $10 a month for 36 months to help Negroes in small businesses and to aid in housing. Two hundred people responded, and the corporation now has 750 members. Many outside the church have requested membership.

Federal funds of over a million dollars were made available to the Zion Nonprofit Corporation to erect one hundred one-and two-bedroom apartments on Girard Avenue between 10th and 12th Streets in Philadelphia to be known as Zion Gardens. These are leased to middle-income families — either white or Negro are welcome — and the proceeds are used to build additional apartment buildings of a similar nature.

This project is typical of Dr. Sullivan's approach: a self-help program. His motto is "We help ourselves." As he puts it, the Negro "controls the purse strings." "I believe," Dr. Sullivan is quoted as saying, "he should be on the building and production end, instead of on the rental end or the buying end of old properties. The people themselves will share in the erection and ownership of housing, utilizing whatever instruments are available, through whatever government programs are available."

The Community Investment Corporation is the first program of the kind in the country. Zion Gardens was the first project in Philadelphia to borrow funds at low interest under the federal housing law. This permits organizations such as church groups to obtain long-term FHA loans at low interest. Low-cost housing can thus be provided for those who cannot afford homes built by private developers, yet are too well off to qualify for public housing. Dr. Sullivan visualizes more garden apartments, housing developments, shopping centers, factories, and industrial complexes. He is a dreamer, but he is one whose dreams have a way of coming true.

"My hope is to build a garden complex each year for the next ten years," he is quoted as saying, "and not necessarily in the colored parts of the city. I'm confident we'll be able to get the land. We'll put up medium-sized apartment houses so that Negroes will be able to be integrated, so I won't have to beg people to let me in." He also said that his first shopping center was under consideration. Several years ago he provided a home for the aged, the Zion Baptist Home on West Tulpehocken Street, in Germantown. Here the old people may sun themselves on terraces, spending their declining years in comfort, with watchful nurses in charge.

In Pennsylvania, a Fair Housing Law guarantees the right of every individual to get better housing for himself and his family, without regard to race, religion, or national origin. It was enacted on September 1, 1961. The Philadelphia law, which became effective June 10, 1963, makes almost identical stipulations. Other states and cities are covered by similar laws. The changes that these housing laws will bring about cause apprehension in the minds of residents where the changes are taking place.

The Commonwealth of Pennsylvania, through the Pennsylvania Human Relations Commission, has made available an excellent leaflet, "Fairness in Housing," which answers the questions of both whites and Negroes. It also mentions other minority groups:

> Many people worry about getting neighbors of a different race, religion or nationality background. The greatest concern of most white citizens is about Negro neighbors, but in varying degrees— depending upon the particular locality—people express fears about Jews, Catholics, Puerto Ricans, Orientals or some other minority group.

The leaflet answers some of the most frequently asked questions:

> "Will the new neighbors take good care of their property?"
>
> Studies have shown that those who move into your neighborhood probably will have about the same income as you do, and the same amount of pride in maintaining their homes. Because they are trying to better their circumstances, members of minority group families often keep up their property in a better than usual fashion.
>
> "Will the new neighbors bring crime and juvenile delinquency to the area?"
>
> No. It is not skin color, religion or ancestry that breeds crime or delinquency. These things are caused by poverty, slum conditions and inadequate police protection.

"If one minority family moves in, will members of that minority soon become the predominant group in the neighborhood?"

Not necessarily. Homes are bought, sold and rented by individual families. No one can move into a house or apartment unless someone moves out. So long as there is no frightened exodus, no drastic change in the composition of the neighborhood will come about. A further fact of importance: the operation of a Fair Housing Law means that some homes in all neighborhoods are available to minority group families without discrimination. This will reduce the concentration in any particular neighborhood.

"Will the value of my property fall if a Negro family moves into our neighborhood?"

Facts learned in a research study of 10,000 real estate sales over a 12-year period in seven cities contradict this myth about housing. The study showed that 41 per cent of the homes in interracial neighborhoods did not change in price, while 44 per cent increased in price by margins ranging from 5 to 26 per cent. The remaining 15 per cent dropped in price by margins ranging from 5 to 9 per cent.

"What about social relationships with the new minority group neighbors?"

Similarity of interests, backgrounds and tastes determine the extent and character of any social relationship. All neighbors, of course, expect and deserve respect, courtesy and a reasonable degree of privacy.

The leaflet discusses what you should do if you see a Negro family looking at a house that is for sale in your neighborhood:

Most important of all is to go about your business as usual and don't panic. The increased cost of buying a home and moving is reason enough for calm, clear thinking. Your best action is to stay put. The most likely way to lose some of the money you have invested in your property is for you and many of your neighbors to put your homes up for sale all at once. This flooding of the market with houses for sale may force some of you to sell at a loss.

In addition, consider this fact: If you sell your home because a Negro family has moved into the neighborhood, you may find that the section to which you move is very likely to receive Negro residents in the not-too-distant future.

The leaflet urges the reader not to take part in any effort to prevent the new family from securing and moving into their new home or apartment, pointing out that it is unlawful to aid anyone in any act forbidden by Pennsylvania's Fair Housing Law.

It also urges that the reader report to the state or local Human Relations Commission and to the Pennsylvania Real Estate Commission any attempt on the part of a real estate salesman to frighten him or his neighbors into selling his home or their homes. The Real Estate Commission is empowered to suspend or revoke the license of a real estate broker or salesman who tries to create panic selling by appealing to racial or religious prejudices.

Some practical advice is offered the reader in the following sensible suggestions:

—Speak up for the right of all people to secure whatever housing they can afford.
—Be willing to sell or rent your property to any family that will be a good neighbor, regardless of race, religion or national origin.
—Instruct your real estate agent to sell without discrimination.
—Make it your business to meet members of the new family and welcome them to the neighborhood.
—Be as friendly and helpful to the new neighbor as you would be to any other neighbor.
—Invite the new neighbor to join in community activities such as the parent-teacher association of the school, the church, civic club and neighborhood improvement program.

As the leaflet points out, "the house and the neighborhood that you live in have a great deal to do with your well-being and the proper raising of your children. Your family deserves a comfortable home, adequate public services and a safe neighborhood with places for your children to play and develop normally. Just as you are entitled — in a democratic free-enterprise system — to the best automobile you can afford, likewise you are entitled to the best quality housing that you can afford. . . . Good housing is a right to which all are entitled as American citizens. . . ."

To this statement might be added the right of children to grow up free from prejudice in an integrated community.

child care
is a key

A SMALL NEGRO GIRL tottered along Columbia Avenue in Philadelphia, past open taverns, threading her way among pedestrians, totally unaccompanied. Two Negro women stood on the curb across the street watching her.

"It's a shame," said one to the other, "that, with five churches in this neighborhood, there's no place for children except the streets when their mothers are away at work."

This indictment does not hold true of all churches and all neighborhoods. Zion Baptist Church, of which Dr. Sullivan is pastor, at Broad and Venango Streets, in this same general area of Philadelphia, has a large day care center which accommodates 65-70 preschool children, ranging

61

in age from three to six years. It opened with six children under the care of Mrs. Utensie Hillian, who is still in charge and heads a growing staff.

Children are kept occupied with free play, toys, puzzles, blocks, a housekeeping corner, and creative art. Four rooms on the second floor are used for some of these activities, while the gymnasium provides a play area and dining room. A visitor to the gymnasium during playtime is reminded of corn popping by the small children hopping up and down with excitement. Outside activities include a large and a small jungle gym, a seesaw, a sliding board, swings, and a sand box.

Children stay in this day care center from seven o'clock in the morning to five-thirty in the afternoon while their mothers are at work. (About two hundred thousand mothers work in Pennsylvania.) A rest period for the children follows a hot lunch, and a light snack breaks the afternoon. About 30 older children come in before school opens, return for lunch, and come back to the day care center after school. They are permitted to come on holidays and during vacations too. Mothers pay for the day care service on a sliding scale based on income and size of family.

Such a program is offered by many churches throughout the city. It is important that churches be committed to this helpful service without invariable expectation of pay. Although it is desirable for families to pay for this service, many cannot afford to do so. Therefore the service has to be financed by the churches in such a way as to provide for both circumstances.

The Board of Education in Philadelphia, which operates some of the child care centers, defines its educational program as one which affords "safe, happy growing-up experiences for children. The arts, music, science, social studies, physical education, all form the vehicle through which children learn to live together in a friendly atmosphere, to understand and enjoy each other's contributions, to share, to work and to play cooperatively in groups with children their own age and to learn about the world in which they live."

This is a broad conception of the child care center. The word "care" has come to mean more than protection from bodily harm, important as that is. It has come to mean more than filling the time with healthful play, though that, too, is a desirable part of the project. The modern child care center is dedicated to "growing-up experiences," to helping children live together in harmony, "to work and play cooperatively," and to "learn about the world in which they live."

Certain ideal standards for child care centers need to be stressed. Centers should be staffed by trained personnel, not just by willing but untrained volunteers. Volunteers are welcome if they are willing to undergo training.

There are three main sources of funds: parents who pay for services, church members in the church-operated centers, and public funds. Adequate space, safe and free from hazards, must be obtainable. In centers operated by the Board of Education, parents are asked to accept some fiscal responsibility, but in general the program is financed by the city and administered by the Board of Education. A scale of fees based on take-home pay and the number in the family is used in determining what the parent should pay. Children like to feel that their parents are providing for their education and care. At any rate, they need to have a parent image of provider, protector.

Outdoor space should be accessible if possible. The location should be convenient for the families concerned.

Increasing emphasis is being placed upon the necessity of adding to the number of centers and improving the quality of existing ones. Strict, rigid discipline is to be avoided — the emphasis is upon good group care under trained personnel, resulting in well-integrated, free, joyous personalities.

Child care centers sponsored by the Board of Education in Philadelphia care for children, both Negro and white, during the long day — eight, nine, ten hours — while their parents are at work. Fifty-five percent of the children have only one parent. Some of them are in the center because of illness — physical or mental — at home.

In addition to its child care centers, the Board of Education sponsors parent nurseries and kindergartens. In the nurseries, parents are required to spend one day a week with the children and to attend evening meetings where home management is discussed. The Board also sponsors Head Start programs during the summer for children who expect to enter the first grade in the fall, and who have had no previous kindergarten experience. Still another project for children is known as "Get Set," designed to help youngsters of three and four to live more richly at their age level. As their teachers take them on trips, they learn that vegetables grow in the ground and fruit on trees, that milk comes from cows, and many similar facts that other people take for granted. Children may be enrolled in this program in churches throughout the city. In all of these programs, children are protected by a thorough physical examination and periodic health checkups thereafter.

One of the thirteen centers operated by the Board of Education in Philadelphia is the Pastorius Child Care Center in the Francis D. Pastorius School at Woodlawn and Sprague Streets. This center, though child oriented, works with the parents too. It attempts to give more than day care; it tries to lay a foundation for later education as well. The Pastorius center has been in operation for a long time; the Board of Education has sponsored child care centers for twenty years and Pastorius was one of the first. Throughout that period the Board has sought to raise standards and expand the program. The need is so great that often a waiting list exists of over one hundred families representing many more children.

Admission to the center occurs only after the prospective family has been carefully screened. A mother must apply in person. The program of the center is then explained to her and she is shown through the building. She fills out an application form, giving information such as her name, address, and size of family. She is given a date on which she is to telephone the head teacher to confirm that she is still interested. If she has not called by that date or within the following few weeks, her name is dropped from the waiting list. If she telephones, she is given another date to telephone again. Then she is asked to come to the center for an in-depth interview, in which she tells all about her child. On the basis of this interview, teachers can anticipate responses.

Then a group of teachers meets with the mother, relating the program to the needs of the family and discussing how difficulties in the child's behavior can be overcome. (Perhaps he refuses to eat or objects to taking a nap.) The mother is encouraged to tell about her own childhood. For example, if she had negative feelings about school, they may have influenced her child.

After this thorough preparation, the child is accepted and is gradually absorbed into the center. A preschool child stays only one and one-half hours the first day, perhaps from nine-thirty to eleven. His mother remains with him all of the time. On the second day he is left in the group and told that his mother will be nearby in the office. She stays close by, filling out the necessary papers. The third day the mother leaves the building; the child stays through the morning and for lunch. On the fourth day he stays until three or four o'clock. The fifth day he may stay even later, though it is not recommended that he stay for the entire time that the center is open — from seven in the morning to six in the evening. This is considered too long a day for so young a child and is avoided if possible. The child's time at the center is dependent upon the length of his parents' working hours, unless arrangements can be made for someone to pick him up and stay with him until the parents return.

A responsible person named by the parents may call for him and take him home. Parents file an escort list of the names of persons who are acceptable to them to bring their children home. All others who present themselves are turned away. Parents may change the escort list from time to time, adding names or taking them off. But all such changes must be made in writing. Some school-age children are allowed to go home alone, if their parents have given written permission. Some reliable person must be at home to receive them. If a child talks to a stranger, or plays along the way, the center investigates.

The wise and capable head of Pastorius Child Care Center is Miss Linda-Ann Smith. Miss Smith says that of the 115 children at present in the center, all but five are Negroes. She says that the family backgrounds of the children show great variety, economically and socially. Parents come from many occupations. Some are teachers, nurses, office and factory workers, city employees, post office workers, dentists, and laborers.

She speaks of the medical care the children receive. After admission to the center, a child is vaccinated and has immunization shots. He is given a medical examination once a year by a doctor. A doctor from the Medical Division of the Board of Education is usually assigned to the child centers. A check is made to see whether the mother has made the recommended follow-up to the medical examination. All the children receive vitamins every day at the center.

They also receive nourishing food. Preschool children have a mid-morning snack of juice and crackers. At noon they are served a hot full-course meal. It is permissible for them to ask for more and to choose second portions. Overweight children are given skimmed milk. Mealtime is intended to be a time of enjoyment.

Preschool children have a nap after lunch every day and are offered milk and cookies when they get up. Most of them are picked up soon after half past three o'clock to go home. School-age children receive milk and cookies at half past four. The menu is varied with crackers and cheese, crackers and peanut butter, and raisins.

The preschool children are divided into two groups: nursery and kindergarten. Nursery children are from three years of age to four and one-half. Kindergartners range from four and one-half to six. At the end of kindergarten, the children are tested as they are in public school kindergartens, before going into the first grade. The nursery group numbers about twenty children; the kindergarten, up to thirty.

Those of school age who spend part of their time in the child care center are also in two groups: junior school age ranges from six years to eight and one-half, and senior school age ranges from eight and one-half to eleven.

Two teachers are in charge of the nursery and two work with the kindergarteners. One teacher in each group must be qualified by a college degree with credits in appropriate subjects. The second teacher must have had two years of college, including certain necessary credits, and must be continuing her education. The junior school children must have one teacher, and the seniors also have one. Approximately thirty children are in each of these groups. Each teacher is on duty eight hours, including lunch time, and salary is commensurate with her training and experience. She eats with the children, but has a break of half an hour away from them. Her vacation corresponds with her period of service, four weeks being the maximum. If she wishes to attend summer school, she may take an additional two weeks without pay.

The head teacher (in this instance, Miss Smith) initiates the program with the children's needs in mind. The program is evaluated at the end of the week when the teachers discuss changes that need to be made, and why, in relation to the behavior of individual children. Developmental records are made every four months. These are used by the teachers, but not given to parents. Information in them is, however, discussed in parent-teacher conferences. Usually the head teacher is included too; in fact, such conferences are almost always three-way meetings. A conference may be called by a parent, a teacher, or the head teacher, whenever a need is felt. Lesson plans are posted in every room, and parents can see that planning is involved. Long-range plans provide for continuity. Questions are asked: What have the children gained? How much have they grown?

The program provides for sensory experiences — seeing, hearing, touching, smelling, and tasting. It presents simple scientific concepts, such as which substances melt, which ones float, and which ones dissolve. The children work with paints, paste, clay, play dough, picture books, and records. They develop motor coordination by climbing, jumping, and swinging; also by using walking boards, tricycles, barrels, wagons, seesaws, large balls, and large hollow blocks. They gain concepts of size and weight from using small unit boxes. They learn, for example, that two half units make a whole one.

They learn to use scissors and tie shoe laces. They dramatize stories, act out problems, play with dolls, and pretend to be firemen. They gain knowledge of language by listening to stories, by telling stories, and by discussing stories. They learn from trips to the zoo and to the fire station. From music they learn bodily movement and rhythm, singing, and dancing. They become acquainted with drums, bells, xylophones, tambourines, and triangles. They develop socially, learning to have self-respect, to care for others' feelings, and to relate to other children and to adults.

In short, they learn in Pastorius how to become well-rounded human beings. The child care center offers them a chance for full development that promises well for the next generation. The quality of the center resides less in its beautiful, modern building than in its teachers and its program. And this one child care center is typical of many others.

foster grandparents
are keys

"GRANDPA'S COMIN' TODAY, Grandpa's comin' today!" chanted four-year-old Ted, jumping up and down with excitement. He could hardly wait to see his friend, his seventy-six-year-old foster grandfather. Together they had worked on a puzzle. Grandfather had had to find most of the pieces, but Ted had enjoyed seeing the picture grow. Today they would finish it, and Ted was watching eagerly from the window to catch sight of Grandfather as he turned the corner.

On August 28, 1965, the White House announced an antipoverty program designed to benefit five and one-half million elderly citizens and at the same time help the children of the poor. In the first stage of the program, 18,200 elderly Americans were employed to aid neglected and retarded children at a cost of forty-one million dollars.

President Johnson was quoted as saying that one-third of all Americans over 65 years old were living in poverty, with an average income of $1,150 a year. He went on to say: "The aged poor have maturity and experience to offer. They are eager to help themselves and others. We are going to use this rich, untapped human resource to help others less fortunate. In turn, it will enable these elderly people to find the dignity and usefulness they seek." This program was financed by an antipoverty appropriation passed by both houses of Congress.

One of the first phases of the federal antipoverty project was called "Foster Grandparents." The elderly (over the age of sixty) served as "substitute parents" for neglected children in institutions. The project was expected to reach into fifty states at the cost of ten million dollars. The first part of the program employed nearly two thousand elderly poor to work with about five thousand neglected infants living in institutions. Twenty-two such projects began in twenty states with two million, seven hundred thousand dollars in grants. Later, another two thousand elderly folks were engaged to help care for two thousand older children in institutions. Other phases of the program trained ten thousand elderly persons as home health aides to bring help and comfort to bedridden, sick, and disabled people.

An estimated twenty-one thousand unwanted or neglected children up to eight years of age are in orphanages, charity institutions, and hospitals. Sometimes one is adopted into a family, but many of them wait in vain for such an event. In the meantime, the elderly can bring the children happiness and cheer. Older people who have love and time to give were sought to minister to these deprived children. They spent four hours a day, five days a week, with them. Pay ranged from $1.25 to $2.00 an hour, according to local wage levels.

Each foster grandparent divided his four hours a day between two children, two hours with each child. This was done for five days, after which a second foster grandparent visited with the child on the other two days of the week. Whenever possible, it was arranged to have a woman as one "grandparent" and a man as the other. It is believed that many older people can give these neglected children a warm emotional experience and the happy companionship with a grownup which is not often found in institutional life. In the cut-and-dried routine of institutions, too few opportunities for such relationships exist.

Older persons selected for service as foster grandparents were given instruction and were paid during the instruction period. They applied at their State Employment Service offices. They were referred to local community agencies which had agreed to sponsor the program. The Foster Grandparents Program meets two crying needs in one operation. It supplements the needs of elderly people, giving them financial aid and also a sense of being wanted and needed. It provides for children and infants the "tender, loving care" without which they can be emotionally scarred for life.

Of course it is important that all foster grandparents be carefully screened to make certain that only those who would be helpful to the children are chosen. With the announced necessary reduction of federal aid to the program it is vitally required that such local organizations as churches, city officials, and city health and welfare councils rally to support it. It is too valuable a project to be lost because of the lack of available funds. Repeated editorials by a prominent radio station have again and again called this important program to the attention of listeners with an appeal for local undergirding of the project.

Some of the foster grandparents who have participated in the program say that it is the best thing that has happened to them since they retired. Some even say that it is the most satisfying, rewarding experience in their lives. Apparently, the program has been a great success wherever tried. Its purpose is to give unwanted children attention, companionship, and love. It is not a babysitting job, nor is the foster grandparent expected to give any physical care. It is a project designed to bring human warmth into the life of a neglected child. The foster grandparent reads to the child, talks with him, and takes him for little walks. In performing such simple services, he not only helps the child but also derives great satisfaction, himself.

If the child and the foster grandparent are of different races, so much the better!

fellowship house
is a key

"FELLOWSHIP ISN'T A PLACE OR A PROGRAM; it's a way of life. Fellowship means living so that despair turns to hope, prejudice to understanding, war to peace, hate to love. Through fellowship you can make a difference; through fellowship you are never alone."

These words appear on the wall of the auditorium in Fellowship House in Philadelphia. They sum up the life that goes on there and in twelve houses of fellowship across the country. These centers, located where the action is, express a way of life.

Long before the emergence of the Civil Rights movement as we know it today, the Fellowship way of life was quietly going on in Philadelphia under the leadership of

Marjorie Penney, now Mrs. Victor Paschkis, who still is head of the House. She came to the movement five months after it was founded in 1931. Ten years later (1941), she moved with it into an old firehouse where the floors were thick with the scum of accumulated dirt. She is at the heart of the present, more adequate, building. Her total service covers more than thirty-five years. Alert, understanding, and gracious, she is a friend to the thousands of children, young people, and adults who pass through the doors of Fellowship House every year.

The present House at 1521 W. Girard Ave., acquired in 1957, is of four stories, with a huge auditorium, dining rooms, lounges, and dormitories. Here the manifold activities of the House go on, with Hindus, Buddhists, Muslims, Catholics, Jews, and Protestants participating. It may be a lecture or a "docu-drama" that summons an audience. Perhaps it is a concert or a program of folk music, or dancing. It may be the annual Passover celebration or a pageant depicting the history of the Negro in America.

> Inside Fellowship House are lights, laughter, human longing, songs and thoughtful silence . . . the happy noise of little children . . . the needed wisdom of hopeful oldsters.
>
> Inside Fellowship House are the biggest problems of our world —how to change hate to love, war to peace, despair to hope, how to do it NOW, in our town—in the South—in Africa—in the tension-torn world.
>
> Inside Fellowship House are the human answers to these problems—people—rich, poor, middle class; colors, many; religions, various—Americans mostly, but some from far away. All of us are learning how to act—how to live—so that our lives can make a difference.

Fellowship House began in 1931 with a few adults, mostly Quakers, and a handful of young people from Philadelphia churches. They had the shared idea that peace must begin at the local level. For ten years, the movement had no home of its own, few friends, and scanty funds, but it kept "hacking away" at the color line. When anti-Semitism became active, Fellowshipers felt that they must take a mighty leap of faith and create a center where people could be trained to deal with crises in human relations. So, in 1941, the old firehouse on Brown Street was acquired and the first Fellowship House in the United States was opened.

The persons that it housed made up not an organization but a *movement*. It comprised the Board, the staff, counselors, volunteers, contributing members, and friends of the Fellowship. The staff numbers about a dozen. The resident staff serves for subsistence: room, board, and clothes. Nonresidents receive tiny salaries. Volunteers give hundreds of hours to help carry the load. Many more are needed.

Each year, twenty-five to thirty young people, known as internes, give three months, six months, or a year without pay, sharing in the work of the House and Farm. It is an exciting and valuable experience. Some of them receive college credit for this work. Fellowship House Farm in the Pennsylvania Dutch country, near Pottstown, Pa., consists of 120 acres. Purchased in 1951, it serves as a summer training center. It is also used for conferences year-round. Every year it has about 4,000 visitors. Many are from Europe, Asia, and Africa. A brochure about the Farm says:

> You'll come away from this farm with some ideas planted in your head. Ideas about people. What are the things that make them what they are. Why there continues to be misunderstanding. How peace and fellowship can be made to take the place of violence and distrust. Ideas about yourself. How you really feel about people of other races and faiths. What you can do right now to help change the world around you. Why it's more and more important for you to speak out, stand up, be counted.

But all is not serious at the Farm. It is a place for fun too. Young people sing folk songs around a campfire, do folk dances in the big barn, browse among antiques, livestock, and food at a Pennsylvania Dutch fair. Art workshops, a swimming pool, drama reading, book reviews, films, and recordings offer diversion.

There is also work to be done. Two or three hours of every day are assigned to interesting work projects. Fields have to be worked, bricks laid, walls painted, flour ground, and bread baked. Everyone helps, and this cooperative spirit keeps the costs low.

Daily seminars and discussions are held on the subject of human relations. Speakers have included Dr. Margaret Mead, Dr. Martin Luther King, Dr. Frank Laubach, and Norman Cousins. Time is allotted to individual and group meditation, periods of silence for reading, and sunset communing on the Hilltop with its 20-mile view.

A four-weeks program of work camping and human relations training draws together young people from diverse racial, religious, national, and socio-economic backgrounds. It is a time for growth, for searching, and for reaching out. It calls for an open heart and an open mind toward all kinds of people and ideas. It asks hard physical work, days brimful of activity and meditation, and a growing relationship with a community of teen-agers, adults, and children.

The comments of some work campers are revealing:

"What I gained most is a feeling of fellowship on the emotional level, not merely the intellectual one. This helps me feel freer in my relations to people. . . ."

"I've heard about returning love for evil and nonviolence, but in that shocking, terrifying, traumatic night when we acted it out, I began to believe it could work. . . ."

"I sat next to a boy — later I found out he was a college senior, and only after we had talked did I actually realize he was Negro. That's the most important part of the Farm. I can intellectualize all I want, but experience is necessary before any real understanding. . . ."

"The Farm changed me so much; afterward I felt like I was inhabiting a completely new person — so much more sure of myself, and more hopeful about everybody else. . . ."

Each day at the Farm has four integral parts: work, study, play, and worship. The period of silence is observed each evening on Hilltop. Of that silence, one young person wrote:

"The experience that was especially significant was Hilltop. Although my religious feeling is usually agnostic, I was very impressed by both the greatness of God and the greatness of man while looking at the natural creation and the human constructiveness that can be observed from Hilltop. . . ."

Fellowship House is not content with its impact upon people who come within its walls and to the Farm for inspiration, however. It reaches out into the community and the city. It offers "Arrow Programs" in Philadelphia and suburban elementary schools, reaching over 6,000 youngsters a year. Staff members and experienced volunteers spend a full week in each school, training children, faculty, and parents in human relations. More than 150 children come in from the streets around the house for weekly instruction in Fellowship. Programs for parents, a preschool nursery, and tutoring are also offered.

Approximately twenty to thirty-five students meet in each of twenty-three Fellowship Clubs in junior high schools each week of the school year. Once a month, delegates from these clubs come together for a General Assembly at Fellowship House.

The High School Fellowship, conducted by the youth themselves, draws teen-agers from public, private, and suburban schools. The program includes study weekends at the Farm, a week-long conference and work camp, monthly newsletters, trips, and speakers. Sometimes high school students help to clean and paint homes in the neighborhood around Fellowship House.

Students from a number of colleges in the Philadelphia area have helped to build and operate the Little Fellowship House at 1710 N. 27th St., Philadelphia, where teen- and college-agers from a ghetto environment are trained in nonviolent action and in serving the local community.

Many related activities have developed through the years as offshoots of the main program at Fellowship House. For example, "Dolls for Democracy," a collection of portrait dolls which began in Fellowship House in 1941, has spread across the nation. Trained storytellers introduce audiences, young and old, through the dolls, to great lives from all races, religions, eras, and countries.

The Fellowship Folk Singers and Dancers give performances in schools, churches, synagogues, and before PTA's and civic groups. Popular Folk Parties feature nationality-group folk artists.

A Women's Workshop meets twice a month for news on the human-relations front and for fund-raising projects. Whole families work to make houses of fellowship of their own homes and to raise children of goodwill. They are called "Families-for-Fellowship."

Study courses and seminars are offered. Each year more than two dozens of courses, conferences, and seminars train hundreds of people of all ages. About half of these are "In-service" credit courses for teachers in the Philadelphia school system. Others include courses for high school students, plus "Incident Control" instruction for suburban communities.

Several special events take place each year. An annual Christmas-Hanukkah party and the Passover Seder are two of many occasions which give people an opportunity to share one another's traditions.

Thousands visit the House and Farm, persons of all ages, on trips and tours. Among them are foreign dignitaries sent by the United States Department of State. The House is also a recruiting center for the Peace Corps.

The twelve houses and groups across the country that are patterned after Fellowship House of Philadelphia are united in a Federation of Fellowship Houses. These warm, vital centers of Fellowship need volunteers who will give time, talents, and money to support the Fellowship "way of life," to turn despair to hope, prejudice to understanding, war to peace, and hate to love. The other eleven houses of fellowship are those at Reading, Pa.; Media, Pa.; Baltimore, Md.; Washington, D. C.; Cincinnati, Ohio; Columbus, Ohio; Knoxville, Tenn.; Kansas City, Mo.; and Paterson, N. J.; plus the Farm at Pottstown and Little Fellowship House at Philadelphia.

Fellowship House numbers some distinguished names among its friends. Among them are Clement Attlee, Ralph Bunche, Judge William H. Hastie, formerly of Jamaica, and Marshall Field III.

education
is a key

ACCORDING TO FIGURES given in the *Statistical Abstract of the United States,* 1966, over two million adults in our country are functionally illiterate — that is, they cannot read or write. These are the people who can sign legal papers only with their "mark," and who often carry a book or a folded newspaper on the street or in the subway to hide their deficiencies. In a country with fine schools, competent teachers, and adequate school supplies, this fact seems incredible.

Methods must be devised to correct these conditions. It must be made possible and attractive for youngsters to stay in school, at least until they learn the rudiments of education. The rate of school dropouts must be lowered.

83

Educators are aware that in school districts where the children are poor, there is a high incidence of dropouts. In 1966, over two billion dollars were allocated by the federal government for educational programs specifically designed for the poor. Federal funds were available, both from the U. S. Office of Education and the Office of Economic Opportunity, for projects in impoverished areas to persons of all age levels.

Preschool children have been greatly helped by Project Head Start, which will be discussed in the following chapter. Older children must be shown the advantages of a job and the necessity for remaining in school to prepare for one. The school counselor can help by organizing visits to offices and factories where the students can see people at work. After such a visit, the counselor explains what wages are, what one must do to receive them, and how one lives better when he earns wages. It is surprising how new to young people of dependent families these ideas are. For example, they know nothing of specialization of jobs. They think merely of "going to work."

Even in the first years of school, it is possible to predict which pupils will be dropouts. As early as the fourth grade, the signs begin to appear, and by the fifth and sixth grades they are plainly visible. So, the earlier the child's preparation for life can begin, both at home and in school, the better are his chances for success.

Certain facts should be borne in mind. First, a teacher's expectation of a child's success or failure in the future should not be determined by his intelligence quotient (IQ). Some teachers expect a child with a low IQ (say of 75) to fail. Yet recent research among prekindergartners has demonstrated that IQ's are changeable. Children with IQ's in the 70's have rapidly risen to an IQ of 100, the norm, and higher. As one author says, "For the child of deep deprivation in his early years, the IQ score is apparently more a measure of his intellectual stimulation than of inborn potential." The teacher who refuses to be discouraged by a low IQ and who has faith in the child's native ability is fulfilling the goal of the teaching profession by helping him to try for and reach the limit of his capability.

Second, reading and skill in spoken language are the foundations upon which knowledge is built. A child may be helped to be sensitive and aware of distinctions among things, colors, and sensations. He then will be able to put his experiences into words. The teacher can help the child to become aware, and his parents may be alerted to the need of exposing him to new surroundings and to communication.

Third, children, especially the underprivileged, need help in learning to listen. A child needs to listen to the sounds of words and relate them to the objects that they identify. A teacher displayed several vegetables to a group of children. "What are these?" she asked. "Vechebas," a girl said. "Vegetables," said the teacher. She then pointed to a tomato. "What kind is this?" she asked. A boy proudly waved his hand. "Tomatah," he replied. "Tomato," said the teacher. "What's this?" "Cair," answered a girl. "A carrot," said the teacher. It is obvious that these children needed to listen. A child needs experience in identifying many sounds around him. He needs to learn to listen to a story and to discuss it. He needs to go on "experience trips," when his teacher emphasizes listening to sounds.

A teacher may record a child's speech on tape and surprise him with some of his poor speech habits. Sometimes he improves remarkably after hearing himself recorded. A child who usually has little to say may be induced to speak into a tape recorder for the sake of the exciting experience.

An interesting, relatively new concept in education is the system of promoting and grouping children according to their individual progress and abilities. This nongrading system offers special opportunities for disadvantaged children. A six-year-old, *according to the national average,* should do first-grade work. But the disadvantaged child falls below that average. Under the new philosophy of grouping, the slow-learning child is not shown up as below his classmates thereby suffering a sense of inferiority. Likewise, the fast-moving child is not held back until his classmates catch up. So his enthusiasm is sustained. The first child need not be delayed a whole year; the second is not forced to skip a grade and miss a year's work.

A California school using this system based upon individual progress has abolished grades one through eight and substituted fourteen levels of curriculum. As soon as a child is ready, he moves to the next level, regardless of age or the time spent on a previous level. He picks up in September where he left off in June. He may be promoted to high school in seven years. He is not permitted to do so in less time, because he might not be socially or physically ready. But he has not skipped any of the work by finishing in seven years instead of eight. Reading ability is the principal factor in determining his readiness to move to a new level, because most other learning is based on it. Of course progress in other subjects, as well as social and emotional development, also enters into the determination.

Some challenging questions are asked in a booklet, *Education: An Answer to Poverty,* published jointly by the

U.S. Office of Education and the Office of Economic Opportunity:

> Can't the level of a child's lessons be dictated by what he individually *needs to learn next*, without reference to time, speed of his schoolmates, or national averages?
>
> Can't he be taught and promoted as required by his own ability, instead of by comparison with others?
>
> Would it not be better for a six-year-old to sit beside an eight-year-old who faces the same academic challenge than to keep him chained to other six-year-olds with whom he has almost nothing in common except the year they were born?

Another new emphasis in education is on "real-life" learning tasks instead of conventional class tasks that often seem artificial and unreal to children. For example, a small city in Illinois experimented with a program for disadvantaged high school students. It combined bold classroom innovations with practical job training and parent involvement. Three goals were set for the classroom: communication skills development, consumer and family skills, and job information. Communication skills include reading, arithmetic, speaking, and listening. Special training is given to classroom teachers in the use of unusual tools for developmental reading, such as short stories, magazines, comic books, and graded reading kits, chosen for their strong motivational content. Children are given a wide choice of reading material, allowed to select their own, and to proceed at their own rate of speed, as in nongraded classes. Individualized attention is given students in arithmetic, speaking, and listening.

Consumer education is very practical, in view of the fact that more than half of the girls marry before they are eighteen. Actual visits to stores are made, to simulate purchasing of furniture, food, and clothing. Extensive practice in ordering from mail-order catalogs is given. Mathematics is applied to household budgeting. Students are driven around to "shop" for a house, with emphasis on size, neighborhood, and price. After returning to the classroom, they calculate mortgage payments and the necessary down payment on their "purchase." They also estimate the personal income that would be needed.

They next "furnish" the house and weigh the cost of furnishings against other possible purchases within their "income." Many students have their eyes opened by this type of arithmetic. Needless to point out, these exercises are more practical than merely practicing with imaginary sums unrelated to everyday life.

Their initiation into the "world of work" has four elements: classroom study, "make-work" in school, real work at the project's training school, and employment for pay in an outside, supervised job, for which school credit is allowed.

Classroom study is concerned principally with vocational information, making use of vocational guidance booklets, materials sent out by nearby companies, and field trips to hospitals, factories, government offices, libraries, and farms. Thus the students get pictures of a variety of jobs which help them to decide on what vocation interests them most.

"Make-work" consists of making articles such as flags, flower arrangements, and ceramics, for sale in school stores. Rewards are given for suggestions that result in increased sales. Participation in delivering handbills for the United Fund and stuffing mailings for a health clinic nearby give the students a sense of making community contributions.

Practical experience is gained by both boys and girls through working in a filling station which the school owns and operates. They study filling station management, maintenance, bookkeeping, and customer relations, earning from 50¢ to $1.25 an hour for practical work.

The final step of the program is paid employment outside of school. Students of ability have earned as much as $2.15 an hour. Jobs are in such institutions as libraries, day care centers, hospitals, and private industry. Students are permitted to work up to three hours a day during schooltime. High school credit is given. Some students attend summer industrial schools to prepare themselves further for full-time jobs upon graduation from high school.

Letters are written to parents, telling them about the project. A family counselor and teachers visit in the homes, and meetings of parents and teachers are held to ensure that all understand the program. Mothers and fathers are invited to go on field trips and are asked to provide transportation for such trips. Parents are invited to speak to students about their work. One father who had a great interest in the community was hired to promote parent participation.

Such a program not only helps the students involved in it, but has great influence on the whole community. Imaginative education of this kind is a key to human progress.

head start
is a key

Senator Edward Kennedy of Massachusetts once related an incident from the Head Start project. When a number of underprivileged children were asked to identify the picture of a Teddy bear, thirty percent of them said "Rat." Sad to say, they were more familiar with rats than with Teddy bears.

A Head Start teacher wanted to read a story about farm animals to her class. She asked if the children all liked milk. They nodded. Then she asked where milk came from. One child answered "Store." Another, "Bottle." None of them knew that milk comes from cows.

Underprivileged children are often unable to identify colors; they do not recognize shapes: blocks, circles, squares. They are not aware of time. Sometimes they do not even know the meaning of such elementary words as "arm" and "leg." Many of them have never seen a book or magazine in their homes. Many of their parents cannot read, though they are native born.

It is to help such children to enlarge their background of experience that Project Head Start was organized under Sargent Shriver's Office of Economic Opportunity. Just as child care centers are intended to care for children of working parents, Head Start classes are designed to prepare children of deprived families for school. They are part of the "War on Poverty," financed by federal funds.

Educators recognize that even in small children signs of later failure and subsequent dropouts from school appear. Little by little, the child senses the difference between himself and his more prosperous schoolmates, a difference that goes much deeper than surface indications such as clothes and homes. The underprivileged child becomes aware that a whole world of knowledge, with which he as a child of poverty is unfamiliar, exists. He is conditioned to failure and headed for unemployment and dependence.

During the summer of 1965, Head Start classes were begun in thousands of school systems across the country. Through them, many four- and five-year-old children were helped to prepare for entry into the first grade that fall. Over 13,000 child-development centers were opened in 2,300 communities throughout the country. Their purpose was to remove some of the handicaps that children from underprivileged homes faced when they entered school. The program aimed to catch such children before their school life even began. The project started with enthusiasm. One hundred thousand full-time volunteers enrolled to staff the 2,300 centers. An additional four thousand part-time volunteers enlisted, to drive cars, read books, tell stories, play games with the children, and help in any way possible.

Many health deficiencies exist among children from low-income homes, such as poor eyesight, dental decay, and undetected tuberculosis. To discover and correct these conditions, fifty thousand doctors, dentists, nurses, and optometrists donated their services. Sargent Shriver commented: "This voluntary outpouring of America's heart to the 559,904 children of the poor who will jump into Head Start in the next few days is the greatest voluntary effort in peacetime this country has ever known."

In Philadelphia, Project Head Start got off to a good beginning with forty-five hundred youngsters in three hundred classes, meeting in 91 schools. Classes lasted for eight weeks. Fifteen pupils were allowed in each class. A certified teacher, a teaching aide, and at least one volunteer were in charge. Verses, songs, finger plays, films, and filmstrips were used. Classes began at nine o'clock and lasted until three, with breaks for a midmorning snack of juice and crackers and a free lunch. Free physical checkups, vaccinations, and polio immunizations were given. The program included trips to the zoo and to historical and cultural institutions.

Two major advances the children make are in the fields of speech and reading. Before attending Head Start, underprivileged children are apt to answer a question with a single word, not a sentence, nor even a phrase. It is usually a general word — the children are not trained to make fine distinctions. At first, the children say little to each other and almost nothing to the teacher. They come from homes where there is very little communication between adults and children. In the Head Start class children learn to communicate with one another and with their teachers. They play with telephones and make tape recordings. They learn to work, play, and live together.

It has long been recognized that reading ability is the key to educational progress. Reading disability, caused by disadvantages in early childhood, cripples the child throughout life. Delores Durkin (Columbia University, Teachers College) has pointed up through her studies the importance of storytelling and other book-related experiences in establishing "reading readiness" in children. A child needs an active imagination, an oral vocabulary, familiarity with books, and the ability to listen before he can learn to read effectively.

Operation Head Start gives preschool children periods of storytelling (sometimes bilingual where the need exists). An effort is made to enlist help in the home. For example, children are encouraged to build home libraries. In the Head Start class, storytelling is combined with browsing through picture books, and occasionally the child is given a good paperback book of his own. His parents, who may have a language barrier, because they are foreign-born, or may not be interested because they are illiterate, must be convinced of the worth of the effort.

The enlistment of parents was found to be comparatively simple. When they were properly approached, they were eager to learn how they might become not only affectionate parents, but wise, intelligent ones. Teachers drew out their interests and abilities and were able to enlist them in a working relationship. Once enlisted, they proved helpful in all the efforts of Head Start. They observed the behavior of their own children and of other children at school. Teachers explained to them the reasons for certain types of behavior and offered suggestions for dealing with them. New attitudes characterized the home, and home environments were altered. A fresh understanding of community problems was shared by teachers and parents. Mothers were helped to plan nutritious meals that they could afford. Parents could see improvement in their children's health as a result of changed menus. This large involvement of parents in Head Start has been one of the program's most conspicuous and constructive features. Cooperation between teachers and parents for the benefit of children is certainly a step in the right direction. A parent-coordinator in one of New York's Head Start programs said: "We have made more progress in six weeks than we have been able to make with parents in four years."

The Head Start coordinators go right into the homes. When a little Puerto Rican boy dropped out of Head Start after a few days, the coordinator went to his home. She found the little boy and his mother in a heatless apartment. At once she called up various city agencies and got emergency action. Then she went to another block to retrieve a three-year-old girl who hadn't come because a woman who usually brought her hadn't appeared.

One Head Start school in New York combined twenty slum children with thirty-two more affluent children whose parents paid $425 tuition for the year for each child. Their teacher said, "Both groups of children will benefit. All will be enriched by playing and learning with kids of different backgrounds."

During the summer of 1965 it was discovered that Project Head Start aided school integration. Sponsors in Hinesville, Georgia, on orders from Washington, tried to merge a white class with a Negro one. The white children promptly went home. In Tampa, Florida, a director of two centers offered special treats for the first three weeks of the program. There were hamburgers and French fries for lunch, parties for parents, and field trips to see the whale at Marineland. Then he announced that, for reasons of economy, he was consolidating the two centers. Only one white child dropped out. What is a parent to say when his child asks why he cannot go back to eat hamburgers and French fries and see the whale?

The Park School in Brooklandville, Maryland, near Baltimore, sponsored a Head Start class of 18 Negro children. The parents of 18 white children from middle-class families who were not eligible for free help from Head Start paid tuition to join the group.

In the South, many Head Start classes were financed conditionally before they became integrated, or were started on a token integration basis. Terms of the condition were that the sponsor make genuine efforts to integrate fully. Projects were checked all summer by inspectors of the Office of Economic Opportunity. In many instances they were able to help to speed the process of integration. Where the director was willing to integrate, but was restrained by the school board, support from Washington came for the director. Few cases of deception were detected. When such cases were discovered, funds were cut off. Six communities refused to accept the integration condition and withdrew from the project. Some communities had no history of integration at all until it was begun by Project Head Start.

Head Start inspectors say that in the nine Southern states for which figures are available, seventy-seven percent of the children attended classes with some degree of integration at staff or pupil level. In seventeen states west and south of Delaware, officials of Head Start estimated that eighty-five percent of the children were in integrated classes. About twenty-five percent of children beginning school in these states in the fall were graduates of Head Start.

Under Head Start more than half a million children have received instruction in group experiences, art, music, and speech, and were given nutritious food, medical care, and physical hygiene. The cost was almost ninety million dollars for the first summer. Funds for the following year, when the program was to be put into year-round operation, were gravely cut and, for a time, the whole program seemed in danger.

New York City said it lacked the space for a year-round Head Start program. Schools unused during the summer are crowded during the winter months. Then, too, there was a shortage of staff. Teachers and college students who had worked during their vacations on Head Start were now busy with regular jobs.

Sargent Shriver seems to regard Head Start as one of the most fruitful projects of the Office of Economic Opportunity. To have lasting value, the three-year-olds, as well as four-year-olds, should have the program. There should also be thorough follow-up into the first, second, and third grades, to insure the permanence of what has been learned and this is to be done. President Johnson, in his State of the Union address, January 3, 1967, spoke of the rich promise of the project and hinted that it should be begun earlier in the child's life, and sustained longer. It needs funds and staffs to continue, as it has begun, a program bright with promise.

operation outreach
is a key

JUST AS FOUR-YEAR-OLDS HAVE the Head Start project to get them ready to begin school, so elementary and secondary school pupils have Operation Outreach. Similar projects have other names in other cities, but in Philadelphia the program is called "Operation Outreach" because it provides additional educational services for pupils from public, private, and parochial schools. It is intended to help families living in twelve "pockets of poverty" areas designated by the Philadelphia Anti-Poverty Action Committee.

In each of these twelve areas, one public school is known as an Educational Counseling and Study Center. These centers are open four nights a week, Mondays through

Thursdays, from 3:45 p.m. to 8:45 p.m. Elementary school pupils attend from 3:45 to 6:15; secondary school pupils from 6:15 to 8:45.

The program is planned to reach fifty thousand families living in poverty in Philadelphia. The Educational Counseling and Study Centers are in areas of North, West, and South Philadelphia, where poverty, family disorganization, and anxiety prevent the ready response of the child to learning and resist the school's efforts to build strong character and encourage questioning minds. Poor families often cannot provide the home conditions, motivation, and encouragement needed by children. Parents often cannot give a child the attention, books, conversation, and supervision that he needs to sustain his interest in school. Often they cannot provide even elementary comforts. A young girl remained at her desk when school was dismissed because of bad weather. When her teacher asked her why she did not go with the others, she said, "It's so cold at home."

Operation Outreach is a well-coordinated system of concentrated services designed to achieve the following aims:

1. Remedy education-retarding deficiencies in the children's environment.
2. Stimulate family interest in education.
3. Bridge the gap between home and school.
4. Augment the existing specialized educational program for children from deprived, disadvantaged areas.

The Educational Counseling and Study Centers seek to provide:

1. A variety of supplementary and enrichment services to children of the poor and their families.
2. Liason activities intended to stimulate and support family interest in education and advancement.

The Center is the location for activities to reach families, recruit children, organize volunteers, and help pupils toward improved school performance. Staff and volunteers put in two two-hour sessions each day, each person aiding ten to twelve children per session. The children are helped to strengthen such fundamental skills as reading and mathematics. They may be tutored in any subject in which they are deficient, such as spelling and English, or be helped with their homework in any academic subject. They may also receive counseling regarding academic progress, school and behavior problems, study interests, and vocational development.

Cultural enrichment is supplied through educational visits, tours, cultural events, and efforts to acquaint pupils with forms of cultural activity with which they are unfamiliar. The Center is equipped with books, children's magazines, educational games, simple art supplies, and aids to homework.

Each Center is in the charge of a supervisor who is a professional person with a knowledge of school library materials and teaching aids. An aide is recruited and trained to assist each supervisor. Tutors are also recruited and trained for each Center. High school juniors and seniors, college students, and graduate school students may serve in this capacity. Adult tutors only are used in the evening. Volunteers escort the children home in the evening, help with trips and attendance at cultural events, and assist the supervisor in whatever way necessary.

To be eligible for the program, a child must live in one of the Community Action Council areas, or in comparable needy circumstances, and must be between grade 4 and grade 12. Parents apply for their child on a prescribed form, indicating the subjects in which he especially needs help. He will be referred to the Center by the principal and teachers in his school.

Home and school coordinators work with the families to assure maximum rapport and to derive whatever support is available for the children. Home and school coordinators are given a brief period of training to prepare them for their work. Their duties are:

1. To receive the names of children from disadvantaged families who can benefit from the services of the centers.

2. To contact the families of children referred, verify the economic status, and assure the attendance of the child, cooperation from parents or guardians, and enforcement at home of the Center's work with the child.

3. Recruit Center aides and volunteers from the local community.

4. Provide liaison between the Center staff and the schools from which children are referred.

Skilled counseling for young people from disadvantaged backgrounds is especially urgent, not only because of their problems but also because of the ever-increasing complexity of college entrance and vocational requirements. Never were close ties between home and school so important. Too often parents are brought in only when there is a crisis. Instead, a close and aggressive program of guidance to help students with study and behavior problems is needed. It is especially important that the child and his family have access to health, medical, psychological, and welfare services, and the counselor will help in this way.

The counseling program of Operation Outreach has two objectives: to reach the families of children, otherwise inaccessible, in the evening, and to make available increased time for counseling of children in Educational Counseling and Study Centers. Duties of counselors are:

1. To receive from teachers and tutors referrals of children with special and serious problems, and to contact these pupils and their parents.
2. To arrange home visits, interviews, and conferences with each pupil and his parents for the purposes of strengthening home and school cooperation and improving the school performance of pupils.
3. To develop motivation in each pupil to remain in school and prepare for higher education or jobs and vocations. The Centers have a relationship with the State Employment Service Youth Opportunity Center to encourage vocational interests and guidance.
4. To refer to appropriate school and recreational agencies.
5. To serve as a speaker, resource person and chairman at designated times for Operation Outreach Staff Meetings and Parent-Teacher Meetings.
6. To interpret the Outreach Program in general and the Counseling Program in particular.
7. To aid the staff in understanding and interpreting children's behavior.
8. To record data obtained as part of a counseling record and to share vital information with the day school and associated community agency personnel.

Counselors are recruited on a voluntary basis from the School District's regular counseling personnel, but are paid. It is estimated that a counselor may advise or visit a minimum of twenty pupils or parents a week. Counselors function under the guidance and supervision of a Coordinator of Counseling Services.

One of the greatest contributions of Operation Outreach

is the development of elementary and secondary level cultural enrichment programs. Poor children, especially, need experiences that show them how richly diversified life is. They need to meet successful people and visit established institutions. They need motivation to lift them to achievements that transcend the poverty and social disability from which they suffer. They often do not receive cultural stimulation at home, and find very limited cultural resources in the poor neighborhoods where they live. They may even, through exposure to inferior and debased cultural forms, be unable at first really to appreciate fine things. Operation Outreach seeks to combat such conditions by an extensive program of tours, visits, and activities.

Its aims are:

1. To broaden the cultural experiences of children and youth by exposure to the fields of art, music, drama, and dance.
2. To acquaint children with major civic and social institutions that contribute to the enrichment of life in the metropolitan area.
3. To motivate children to aspire to the best in cultural and social life.
4. To provide experiences that will broaden vocational horizons.

Cultural experiences are not limited to fine arts, but include many public and social events. Parents are encouraged to participate in the program and enjoy the experiences with the children. Some of the experiences sponsored by Operation Outreach are: visits to museums, concerts, exhibits, plays, recitals, dedications of buildings and of art works, airports, rail traffic control centers, food distribution centers, the Italian market, a textile institute, farms, dairies, selected manufacturing plants, newspapers, architects' offices, historical sites, skyscraper offices, auctions, Ukrainian Nationals soccer games, Chinese New Year festivities, San Juan Bautista celebration, a cricket match, a fashion show, a sportsmen's show, a travel agency, scientific laboratories, a weather station, a television studio, an oil refinery, a water filtration plant, the police academy, the central post office, a cartography company, a commercial artist's studio, and City Council.

Children are assembled at the Centers on evenings or weekends, transportation by bus to the events or activities scheduled, and returned to Center locations. Teachers and volunteers accompanying the children are paid for the service.

For many years educators have been aware that ability to read was fundamental to the acquisition of knowledge. It has been evident for a long time that there is a great need for remedial reading assistance. For twenty-five years a reading adjustment teacher in elementary schools has struggled with the problem, and several years ago a city-wide secondary remedial reading program was established, involving every junior, senior, and technical high school in Philadelphia. But it was impossible to reach all pupils in need of remedial help because of the limitations of the School District budget. Now Operation Outreach provides remedial instruction in reading for appproximately one thousand children.

The program seeks to offer remedial reading classes above and beyond those that the school provides during the regular school day. The objectives of the program are to stimulate interest in reading, to motivate pupils to improve in reading, to assist older students in reading materials related to vocational opportunities, to identify and give specific help to pupils of high potential, and to offer a limited amount of psychological testing to discover causes of severe reading retardation.

In the selection of students to receive this help, preference is given to the child who reveals potential by both subjective and objective measurements. The child's motivation is of the utmost importance. Many older pupils are eager for help which enables them to read about vocational possibilities. Operation Outreach offers an opportunity for the pupil with potential and motivation. He can be helped to transcend poverty and overcome the lack of advantages.

⊁ Several experiments are being tested in a few of the Centers to help children become actual *participants* in cultural experiences rather than merely observers. The child discovers that he has talents and his self-image and prestige are thereby enhanced. A dance program, offering instruction in ballet, tap, interpretive, and modern dance, has been started and has proved successful.

A program of creative and expressive art under a qualified instructor introduces pupils to various art media and teaches them harmonious use of color. A worthwhile by-product is the feeling of pride that comes from accomplishment. Still another venture is in the area of creative drama. This project helps establish good speech patterns. By developing a need for adequate speech and providing a reason and opportunity for speaking, the remedial reading program is enhanced. The creative drama group actually creates its own plays, as well as produces them. Music instruction takes two forms: instrumental and vocal.

Operation Second Chance, an after-school tutoring program, has the following objectives:

1. To encourage potential dropouts to remain in school, make up subject failures, and graduate.

2. To attract former dropouts to return to school by offering them a flexible program which will enable them to accelerate the making up of their subject deficiencies.

The use of the Philadelphia Tutorial Project, a non-profit corporation, organized under the laws of the Commonwealth of Pennsylvania, is being successfully tried in Operation Outreach. It provides the Centers with 200 tutors and receives funds in return for their services.

These are some of the programs, projects, and goals of Operation Outreach, which is designed to break the ugly cycle of hopelessness and poverty. It offers counseling on an individual basis to every child enrolled in the Outreach Center. This cannot be done in day school, for the great numbers will not permit it. Where else can a child get this one-to-one social casework experience with veteran personnel who are familiar with health, welfare, and recreational facilities? Where else can he have as good a chance to make something of himself?

the church
is a key

ONE SUNDAY IN THE FALL OF 1965 two Negroes entered the Presbyterian Church in Tuskegee, Alabama, and took seats at the rear of the sanctuary. Everyone had expected that they would come sooner or later, and most of the "private schoolers" (segregationists) had said they would not resist if the Negroes came in "a true spirit of worship." But it happened to be Communion Sunday on which these two came, and that circumstance complicated things. A "private schooler" passed the bread and did not serve the Negroes. A "public schooler" (integrationist) passed the wine and served them.

The minister, Rev. Robert D. Miller, stood quietly until the private schooler returned with the tray of bread.

Then he took it, walked to the back of the church and served the Negroes. This event took place in profound silence. But Tuskegee dinner tables buzzed with conversation about the pastor's action. Soon afterward, Mr. Miller left for a pulpit in Tampa, Florida. He was the third consecutive minister who left — or was dismissed — from the church in the midst of dissension over race.

Of all organizations, the Church of Jesus Christ is the one where love and brotherhood should be made manifest. Yet we have the strange phenomenon of black worshipers being turned away from the doors of some white churches. Some Negro worshipers who *are* admitted are either ignored or only coolly recognized by some white members of the congregation.

Our Lord prayed that all of his followers might be one. Paul wrote to the Galatians: "For as many of you as were baptized into Christ have put on Christ. There is neither Jew nor Greek, there is neither slave nor free, there is neither male nor female; for you are all one in Christ Jesus" (Galatians 3:27-28).

At an annual meeting of the American Baptist Convention, the following resolution was adopted: "We recognize that any form of segregation based on race, color, or ethnic origin is contrary to the gospel of Jesus Christ and is incompatible with the Christian doctrine of man, and with the nature of the Church of Christ. Whenever and wherever any of us as Christians, individually or collectively, denies this by action or inaction, we betray Christ and the fellowship which bears his name."

The resolution goes on to state the belief that all churches in the American Baptist Convention — their membership, leadership, ministry, and staff — should be open to all followers of Jesus Christ, and that every congregation should offer its ministries to all persons in the community.

All churches are urged to support federal, state, and local civil rights legislation providing for:

1. the equal and unhindered right of every qualified person to register and vote
2. the development of and equal access to quality integrated education
3. equal opportunity for employment, union membership, apprenticeship, job training and management promotion undergirded and supported by fair employment practice legislation
4. complete and equal access to all public accommodations
5. all housing in every neighborhood open to everyone without regard to race, religion, or national origin

These are the stated principles of one large denomination. Other denominations have expressed similar views and have passed analogous resolutions. It is to be recognized that such resolutions express the most favorable attitude and that this attitude is shared only in varying degrees by the individuals in the churches.

The members of the churches need only recall and practice the principle set forth in the Declaration of Independence: "We hold these truths to be self-evident, that all men are created equal. . . ." It is indeed a paradox that a country that claims to be the home of freedom and has given freedom to oppressed peoples from many lands should have in its midst a people that have lived within it for generations who must still fight and demonstrate in an attempt to gain their fundamental human rights, such as the vote. The same quest for freedom which was enunciated in Philadelphia and was defended at Gettysburg, the

Argonne, and Iwo Jima motivated the marchers in Selma, Chicago, and Washington. The church has quite properly taken its place with the marchers, for patriotic as well as Christian reasons.

Many white churches in mixed neighborhoods have occasional Negro visitors. Such visits provide the white members with an opportunity to greet the Negroes warmly and ask them to come again. They can invite women visitors to come to the next meeting of the Women's Fellowship and to join a circle. They can suggest the church school for the children of young families. It is important for the visitors to get an impression of a warm, friendly, Christlike church in which they can feel welcome.

It is also important that the welcome not be tinged with a patronizing air. Accustomed to rebuffs and condescension, Negroes are sensitive to any insincerity.

Some churches have received so many Negro members that they are truly integrated churches. Others are integrated because of the merger of a white church and a Negro church. Ideally, it is then no longer considered either a Negro church or a white church, but the church of Jesus Christ. When Negroes and whites are fellow church members and serve together on church boards and committees, they frequently come to know and like one another without barriers of prejudice. Sometimes real friendship and an exchange of hospitality in homes results.

The integrated church calls for more than mutual respect and love. It calls also for the mutual sharing of responsibility and work. When both white and Negro men and women are responsible for a church assignment, such as serving communion, preparing a church fellowship dinner, or organizing a church school of missions, everyone should share in the work that is involved, rather than leave the bulk of it to two or three who can always be counted on. Work, too, must be integrated.

Similarly, all should share in the financial support of the church. Neither must this responsibility be left to a loyal few. Every member, white or Negro, must be helped to see that he must not accept the privileges of church membership without contributing to its support.

A pastor of one integrated church reports that he senses in his congregation a genuine willingness to work together and observes that his church members actually do work cooperatively, both Negro and white. He also counts as an asset the warm friendship of the members for the pastor. On the other side of the ledger, he is aware of the hesitancy of white families with children to join his church, probably because they have a strong feeling against interracial marriage. He also observes a distinct class separation between middle-class Negroes and poor Negroes, and an unconscious tendency on the part of some whites to dominate.

Another minister of an integrated church also speaks of the cleavage between middle-class Negroes and underprivileged ones. He says that no difficulty arose in getting whites and Negroes to *worship* together, but social life is another matter. He, too, attributed the problem of getting them together for social life to the fact that both Negroes and Caucasians are disturbed about the possibility of intermarriage.

One minister who saw one hundred white families leave his church within eighteen months said, out of his sad experience, that when the church became ten to twenty percent Negro, white families began to move out. His disturbed congregation fell into three categories: those who left at once, those who refused to be driven out, and those who chose to remain and work with the Negroes. At present, ten white families commute from the suburbs to attend church school because they want their children in an integrated Sunday school. They refuse to be alarmed by percentages. But when their children are of dating age, even they may leave.

Sometimes it is the Negroes in integrated churches who are disturbed by percentages. They think that a church made up of 60% whites and 40% Negroes is all right, but they are not happy when it becomes 20% white and 80% Negro. The minister said that sometimes integration was for just a transitional period after which the membership became totally Negro and the integration process was shifted elsewhere.

One pastor spoke of the Negro's contribution to the integrated church. The Negro is basically a spiritual person. God is very real to him. He believes in life after death. He expresses his faith in song. In short, he adds conviction, joy, warmth, and color (other than that of his skin) to the church of which he is a member. He does his fellow church members good. This pastor spoke of his own joy in serving an integrated church, the joy of seeing people as God's children, whatever their color.

In one integrated church a diversified group were asked how integration was working in their church. Their frank opinions were interesting and revealing:

1. Quite a meaningful experience — very successful. The problems seem to be a disparity in the leadership potential and the difference in ages. The leadership potential of the Negroes excels that of the whites. The whites are much older chronologically. The relationship is better than in a merger of two churches of the same racial makeup.

2. We are surviving. I do not feel that we have been successful except for holding our own. There is more concern expressed from the pulpit about making the biracial experience work and the problems incidental to our differences, and not enough attention being given to some of the real problems which naturally confront the members of any Christian congregation.

3. I feel fully accepted. People seem very much pleased. I, personally, am pleased to be part of the whole. Visitors seem amazed at the successfulness of the merger. It is getting along well. I am enjoying it.

4. It is a beginning in the right direction, helping people to see the falsity of the stereotyped images they have of each other. People are seeing each other as just people. Some strangeness is still apparent. It demonstrates a willingness to tackle a great social problem.

5. I have forgotten we are integrated. It is a wholesome experience, though not "taking" 100%. I sense no white and colored tenseness. I am at ease.

6. The future is doubtful because most of the white members are older than the Negro members. I am glad we did it. There are no ill feelings. The merger took place at just the right time.

7. We are moving along quite naturally as human beings. The experience helps one to understand people.

8. It is an experience that had to come about sooner or later, one for the better. I enjoy it very much.

9. I feel nothing especial about it. It is a typical church with typical problems and typical people. I wish we could begin to draw more people.

10. I am kind of mixed up about the whole thing. In a sense some things are working out, and some are not. Some things are being done, seemingly just to try to make the experiment work, rather than with genuine sincerity.

using the keys

NOTHING IS MORE USELESS than a key in someone's pocket or lying on a table. But in the hand, inserted in a lock, it becomes very important and valuable. The same is true of the keys presented in this book. The fact that they exist means little unless we take them in our hands, so to speak, and use them. We will find many that we can use, if only we will.

Consider the key which is the "image." Perhaps we need to alter our self-image. We may, when we take a good, long, hard look at ourselves, find ourselves prejudiced, narrow, patronizing, antagonistic. The image may need changing. We may need to change our image of others, as well. Perhaps we need to alter our conception of Negroes, or our image of whites. Perhaps we need to look again at Southerners, at Northerners. Most important of all, we must examine the Christian church, our church, ourselves as church members, and see whether we are projecting an image that is truly Christlike.

We have resources which we can bring to these "key" projects. We have time. Each of us has twenty-four hours a day. We can spend them all on ourselves, for self-improvement, recreation, and the like; or we can devote some of them to one or more of these keys. We could find something to do as a volunteer if we offered some of our time to OIC, or AAE, or the nearest child care center. We might find it necessary to spend some time in training before beginning the actual service. Those of us who qualify could become foster grandparents, spending four hours a day for five days, brightening the lives of neglected children in institutions. We could give time to work in our churches, that the churches might lead, rather than follow, in the solution of some of the pressing problems of the day.

We also have talents as resources. How much we could offer the underprivileged if we could exchange talents with them! And how much they could give us! For example, a shared evening of instrumental or vocal music would not be too difficult to arrange.

Perhaps we have experience and talents that qualify us to fill vacancies that are unmanned, thereby seriously handicapping youth. Some are teachers or former teachers. Others are mature, experienced people who are qualified to teach by degrees that they hold. Why not become desperately needed substitute teachers in elementary or secondary schools? A letter recently sent to members of the Philadelphia Branch of the American Association of University Women reads as follows:

"Many of you have participated in the discussions on public education. We too often love discussion, but do not follow through with action.

"The plight of our schools is reflected in the teacher shortage. Quality education is an empty phrase if classrooms cannot be manned by quality teachers.

"Our teachers are good, but there are not enough of them.

"What real 'grass roots' effort have you made to correct this? Have you offered your time and talent, your concern, to the classroom where the struggle for education really *is?*

"Are you willing to leave your suburban home, or your mid-city apartment to report to a North or South Philadelphia school at 8:45 and teach until 3:00 or 3:30?"

This sort of action expresses real concern and dedication to the ideal of education, which we profess to believe is a *key.*

Of course, opportunities for the use of talents in the church are practically unlimited. All we need to do is to survey the needs and our own abilities and decide where our talents can best be used.

Then there is the great resource of money. Some of us have more of it than others, but all of us should devote a generous share to the church and to worthwhile programs and projects such as those presented as keys in this book. In computing our annual income tax, it is surprising how many of us use the tax table. Of course that may be merely for convenience. But if the ten percent deduction which is automatically allowed by the tax table really covers our medical and dental expenses, taxes, and contributions, it is clear that the percentage of our contributions is limited to a trivial amount.

We sometimes become weary of repeated appeals for money. When we feel that way, we should remind ourselves that God is the source of our money. He gives us strength, health, and intelligence with which to earn it, and we owe some of it to causes which accomplish his will in the world.

We can use the vote too. We can vote for far-reaching, forward-looking legislation that will work toward giving every man his God-given rights. We can write our senators and representatives, urging them to take the right, or what seems to us to be the right, stand on current issues. We can help those who have recently acquired the vote to understand how important it is to use it. It is a key in their hands.

We can practice fair housing, not only supporting legislation to undergird it, but refusing to draw a color line if we have property to rent, or refusing to panic if a Negro moves into the neighborhood.

A pastor of an integrated church recently said, "We can only do it on a 'one-to-one' basis. It can only be done by people who care." His wife took him seriously. She made contact with a Negro family that lived across the street. The mother supported her six children as best she could, too proud to accept relief. The minister's wife took the children into her home after school before their mother returned from work, fed them, bathed them, sewed for them, and had them and their mother to supper on Christmas Eve. She really took to heart the "one-to-one" theory. As time went on, she helped each child to get into a suitable school, in line with his interests and abilities. She tutored them in spelling and arithmetic. One of the girls had a crippled foot. The minister's wife took her to a clinic, where it was decided that an operation was necessary. A tendon was cut, so that the little girl would no longer have to walk on her toes, but could put the heel of her foot down. One-to-one relationship? Oh, yes, and how we wish there were more of them! "As you did it to one of the least of these . . . you did it to me" (Matthew 25:40). And it can only be done by *people who care.*

acknowledgments

THE AUTHOR IS DEEPLY INDEBTED to many people who have supplied ideas and facts and have granted interviews. The idea for this book was born during a significant workshop of the American Association of University Women held in the Free Library of Philadelphia on January 5, 1965, when Dr. Leon H. Sullivan was a speaker. This group was under the leadership of Mrs. Frederick P. Gruenberg, and the coordinator of the workshop was Miss Marie A. Davis, of the Library. Help has been given by the Reverend Elder B. Hicks through his article, "Changing the Image," in *Crusader,* June, 1965. Assistance has been given by several on the staff of Opportunities Industrialization Center, including Frederick E. Miller, Ronald

W. Howard, Clarence J. Boxdale, Clarence Jones, and, especially Albert F. Mitchell, who provided the factual material on OIC. Mrs. Philip Hammer, of Washington, D.C., a trustee of the League of Women Voters Education Fund, granted a helpful interview. Russell B. Barbour, representative of the Human Relations Commission in Philadelphia under the Department of Labor and Industry of the Commonwealth of Pennsylvania, was exceedingly kind in supplying leaflets and information in regard to housing. A pleasant and useful interview was granted by Miss Marjorie Penney (Mrs. Victor Paschkis) at Fellowship House. Mrs. William J. Heydrick, of the Council of Churches of Greater Philadelphia, made constructive suggestions as to possible interviews. Miss Frances M. Becker, director of Education for Young Children under the Philadelphia Board of Education, outlined projects such as child care and Head Start. Mrs. Utensie Hillian gave details of the day care center at Zion Baptist Church. The work of the Pastorius Child Care Center was described by Miss Linda-Ann Smith, head teacher. Samuel W. Watts, Jr., director of Operation Outreach under the Philadelphia Board of Education, was also helpful. Two Germantown ministers, Dr. W. Hamilton Aulenbach and Rev. Hal B. Lloyd, made suggestions used in the chapter on the church, and Howard D. Pindell aided in gathering material for that chapter. News and feature stories published in The New York *Times,* The Philadelphia *Inquirer,* and The Philadelphia Evening and Sunday *Bulletin* were extremely helpful as source material.

To all of these and others who cooperated in the preparation of this book, grateful thanks are expressed.

H. K. W.

index

THE AUTHOR

Helen Kingsbury Wallace is a writer of wide experience and deep perception. A resident of Philadelphia, one of the first cities to experience the racial violence of the 1960's, she made it her purpose to study what is being done in her city and elsewhere to deal with some of the basic problems involved in the current crisis. *Keys in Our Hands* is the report of her extensive reading and interviews in this field.

Miss Wallace is the author of seven previous books and approximately fifty magazine articles and stories. She has served on the faculty of Franklin College, Hofstra University, and Maryland College for Women. She was a member of the editorial staff of the *Encyclopedia Americana*. She also directed the Christian Authors' Guild sponsored by the American Baptist Convention.

She has been a leader in numerous civic and professional organizations including the Religious Public Relations Council, American Association of University Women, the Women's University Club, and the National League of American Pen Women, and has traveled extensively in North America and Europe.